THE MANY FACES
OF DECEIT

THE MANY FACES OF DECEIT

OMISSIONS, LIES, AND DISGUISE IN PSYCHOTHERAPY

by
Helen K. Gediman, Ph.D
and
Janice S. Lieberman, Ph.D

JASON ARONSON INC.
Northvale, New Jersey
London

Production Editor: Judith D. Cohen

This book was set in 11 pt. Berkeley Old Style Medium by Alpha Graphics of Pitts-field, New Hampshire and printed and bound by Book-mart Press of North Bergen, New Jersey.

Library of Congress Cataloging-in-Publication Data
Gediman, Helen K.
    The many faces of deceit / omissions, lies, and disguise in psychotherapy / by Helen K. Gediman and Janice S. Lieberman.
        p. cm.
    Includes bibliographical references and index.
    ISBN 1-56821-592-4 (alk. paper)
    1. Deception. 2. Psychotherapist and patient. 3. Truthfulness and falsehood. 4. Impostors and imposture. I. Lieberman, Janice S. II. Title.
    [DNLM: 1. Psychoanalytic Therapy. 2. Lying. 3. Humanities. WM 460.6 G295m 1995]
    RC569.5.D44G43 1995
    616.89'17—dc20
    DNLM/DLC
    for Library of Congress   95-18353

Manufactured in the United States of America. Jason Aronson Inc. offers books and cassettes. For information and catalog write to Jason Aronson Inc., 230 Livingston Street, Northvale, New Jersey 07647.

To our sons,

Paul Henry Gediman

Mark Spencer Lieberman

Evan Scott Lieberman

CONTENTS

ILLUSTRATIONS

ACKNOWLEDGMENTS

Over the past decade, we have been working independently of each other on various aspects of deception in psychoanalytic treatment and in the arts. In our efforts to bring together our individual works, we have enjoyed the rewards of mutual collaboration in our attempts to unify our originally separate labors by creating in this book a new look at our topic. At every step of the way, both of us, first separately, and then together, were fortunate to have the support, encouragement, and critical input of many to whom we are indebted.

We would like to extend our deepest thanks and gratitude to Dr. Barbara Stimmel, whose encouragement, good wishes, and critical reading of our manuscript contributed greatly to this project. We would also like to thank our publisher, Dr. Jason Aronson, for his enthusiasm and support, and Judy Cohen, Senior Production Editor at Jason Aronson Inc., for her careful work and efficient expediting of the production of this book.

Many colleagues have helped each of us in our work on earlier drafts of papers that were expanded or otherwise modified to form some of the chapters in this book, and have served as discussants at their presentations at professional meetings. We should like separately to express our gratitude to them.

Helen K. Gediman wishes to thank the following individuals who served as discussants at formal presentations of papers that formed the background for some of the chapters in this book: Dr. Charles Brenner, who discussed her paper on imposture at the Association for Psychoanalytic Medicine in 1983; Dr. Edward Weinshel, who discussed a later version of that paper at The American Psychoanalytic Association in December 1984; and Dr. Sheldon Bach, who discussed her "M. Butterfly" paper at the 1990 meeting of Division 39 of the American Psychological Association.

Dr. Gediman thanks Dr. Joseph Lichtenberg, who invited her to publish her paper on supervision and imposture in a 1986 issue of *Psychoanalytic Inquiry*. She is also grateful to Dr. Gerald Fogel for inviting her to print her point of view on the Masson–Malcolm controversy in an issue of the 1985 *American Psychoanalytic Association Newsletter*, parts of which are also included in this volume in modified form. She is indebted to Dr. Joseph Grayzel who encouraged her to write up her first thoughts on the play *M. Butterfly*, and who devoted considerable time and effort to critical readings and commentary on many early drafts of the paper that later, in 1993, was published by invitation of Drs. Donna Bassin and Adria Schwartz, editors of a special issue of *Psychoanalytic Psychology* on the topic of sex and gender in psychoanalysis.

Janice S. Lieberman would like to thank for their helpful comments on the various drafts of papers that emerged as chapters in this volume: Mrs. Suzanne Yaffe Kaplan, Dr. Naama Kushnir-Barash, Mrs. Judith Levitan, Dr. Joseph Reppen, Dr. Arlene Kramer Richards, and Dr. Carlos Saba. She would also like to express her appreciation for their encouragement and support of her written work to Dr. Steven J. Levitan, Dr. Arnold Richards, and Dr. Mark Silvan.

Special thanks are due Dr. Lieberman's colleagues at the Whitney Museum of American Art: the Docents, the staff of the Library, and especially Mrs. Linda Daitz, who has served as a mentor to her efforts in applied psychoanalysis.

Various colleagues have served as discussants at formal presentations of earlier versions of papers that were expanded and modified to be included in the chapters of this book, and their comments have greatly enriched her understanding of the "many faces of deceit": Dr. Moss Rawn, at the 1993 meeting of Division 39 of the American Psychological Association; Dr. Cecilia Karol, at the 1991 meeting of the International Psychoanalytic Association; and Dr. Robert Gillen, at the 1993 meeting of the International Psychoanalytic Association.

Finally, we thank each other for the joys and pleasures of collaboration that eventuated in the publication of this book.

1

THE UBIQUITY
OF DECEPTION

Men are so simple, and so much creatures of circumstance, that the deceiver will always find someone ready to be deceived.

—Machiavelli, *The Prince*

It was a rainy day, the kind that made the analyst feel fortunate that she had a home office. Her first patient, a young woman in her twenties, was late, and the analyst, while waiting, looked out of her window at the street. A taxi arrived at the front door of the apartment building. She saw her patient get out of the taxi, rather regally allowing the doorman to escort her into the building, sheltering her with an umbrella. Two minutes later, she arrived at the analyst's door. She apologized to the analyst for being late. She could not find a taxi—all were taken—and she had to walk twenty blocks to her session in the pouring rain.

Deception is ubiquitous in everyday life. This assertion has been confirmed through discussion, debate, and systematic study by philosophers, theologians, educators, psychologists, and psychiatrists (for example, see Feldman and Ford 1994, Lewis and Saarni 1993, Lieberman 1995, Nyberg 1993). Despite its ubiquity, however, psychoanalysts have not studied deceptive phenomena systematically or comprehensively, although a scattered literature on the subject does exist. We aim to expand upon this literature and to develop a psychoanalytic understanding of how deception in its many varieties serves multiple functions for both the deceiver and the deceived.

This book is concerned primarily with the varieties of deception manifested by patients with their analysts in the treatment situation. *Analyst* refers to one who has been trained in classical psychoanalysis and who conducts both psychoanalytic psychotherapy and psychoanalysis. The psychoanalytic enterprise, because of its inevitable focus on the varieties of illusion and disguise inherent in psychodynamic equilibrium, facilitates and makes accessible conflicts around authenticity among patients and among those trying to understand and treat them. In Part II, in which we deal with deception in the arts, clinical analyses of imposture in a noted artist (Arshile Gorky) and in a character from the drama *M. Butterfly* are presented.

Central and crucial to our position is the belief that deception manifests itself not just individually, but as a dyadic, interactive, relational process, involving not just the false communication of a deceiver but also a receptive Other who responds to that communication and person. This Other's reactions—belief or disbelief—are partly induced by the deceiver and partly by the personal storehouse of unconscious identifications and fantasies that touch on particular deceptions to which he or she is vulnerable.

There is now a sparse but growing body of commentary on deception in the psychoanalytic literature, particularly the work of Abraham (1925), Deutsch (1955), Fenichel (1939), Greenacre (1958a,b), and more recently Finkelstein (1974), Weinshel (1979), Gottdiener (1982), Blum (1983), Gediman (1985a,b, 1986), (Meloy, 1988), Kernberg (1992), Lieberman (1991a,b,

1993a,b), Schreier (1992), Schreier and Libow (1993), and La Farge (1994). No one work attempts to systematize deception in its many variations or to pull together the various account- ings for its operation in the lives of patients in and out of the psychoanalytic situation. That is our goal. We believe that there is something inherently threatening to some psychoanalysts in the notion that their patients may, upon occasion or even often, lie to them consciously and that they may be completely unaware of these lies, or of the sadism and aggression bound up in them, for weeks, months, years (or forever). As a result, although lying and other forms of deception, such as omissions and secrets, are believed to be ubiquitous in treatment (as are transference and resistance), and when instances of deception on the part of pa- tients are reported in case seminars, study groups, or at larger meetings, these instances are not focused upon as having particular meaning, unique and different from other phenomena that result from the compromise formation between wish and defense. When one of us was a candidate and tried to raise with her supervisor the question of why her patient lied, she was countered with a question asking why did she even treat a patient who lied!

We aim to address the important role of aggression in the analytic encounter. Deception and imposture involve a signifi- cant degree of sadism, and individuals suffering from these char- acter disturbances often struggle with conflicts that relate not just to sadism but to narcissism as well. Bach (1994) also notes that the beating fantasies of his perverse patients, although origi- nating in the anal phase, often reflect earlier problems of sepa- ration-individuation. Their sadomasochistic relationships with others defend against childhood loss and trauma. We have found that those who consistently deceive deliberately in the therapeu- tic situation *pervert* and *subvert* the relationship for essentially sadomasochistic gratification. This gratification predominates and serves as a resistance to the analytic work, rendering it mean- ingless at times. They *use* the analyst rather than *make use of* his or her interpretations. The analyst's task is to understand and encourage motivations to abandon gratifications that interfere with the more psychoanalytically valued gratifications: for example, finding out what is truly ailing the patient, helping him or her get better and to have healthier relationships with new figures and with the analyst—the usual goals put forth at the onset of treatment. This task is undermined by the deceptive patient, whether neurotic, character-disordered, or suffering from the psychopathology of everyday life in the average analytic dyad.

Individually and together we have been thinking and writing about these issues for many years, and we are grateful for the recent work done on perversion (Chasseguet-Smirgel 1981, Fogel 1991) and the perverse transferences (Bach 1994, Reed 1994, Renik 1992) that has informed our work.

To repeat, sadomasochistic fantasy and perversion are important factors in some deceptive transferences. Those who deceive their analysts often wish to use and manipulate them. Further along in this book, we discuss the difference between the *perverse transference*, in which an unconscious fantasy denying some aspect of reality is involved, and the *deceptive transference*, which involves a behavior (the false communication to the analyst) that consciously denies or distorts some aspect of reality. There is a difference between looking away from reality and an action deliberately aimed at changing another's perception of reality.

We attempt to classify and explicate the dynamics of various forms of deception—both the positive and adaptive, and the negative and pathological—as they occur in the psychoanalytic treatment situation. We ourselves present our readers with what we regard as an adaptive, positive form of deception commonly used by authors of psychoanalytic books and papers: the disguise of our patients' identities and the omission of material that would give our readers any clues as to who they truly are. Unlike certain deceptive patients, however, we *inform* our readers that we are being deceptive in this way! We confine ourselves to deceptive behavior in the range of personalities and psychopathologies found among patients typically coming to present-day psychoanalytic psychotherapy and psychoanalysis. The patients we are writing about are ambulatory, function generally in a more or less satisfactory manner, and have come to treatment in order to progress further in love and/or work or to deal with some debilitating symptom(s) and/or character traits.

Ideally, the psychoanalytic enterprise is one of mutual truth seeking. But there is a paradox in the way an analyst must listen to patients. The analyst's role involves the suspension of disbelief, but at the same time requires a healthy degree of skepticism that what is being said represents the whole truth and nothing but the truth!

Psychoanalytic treatment is often quite expensive and time consuming. It therefore could seem paradoxical that patients lie to their analysts or omit telling them what might enable them to genuinely help them. We aim to show that there are sound reasons for both the analyst's paradoxical stance in discerning the truth and the patient's paradoxical use of deception to get to his or her inner truths. We aim to explicate the varieties of conscious and unconscious psychic pleasures and gains that serve adaptive, defensive, libidinal, aggressive, and other needs as well as various functions in the personality as a whole. In this way, we demonstrate the various gains, and not simply the more obvious costs and losses that the analytic patient gets out of deceiving the very analyst he or she is paying to help him or her. These psychic gains and pleasures seem to override the need to get better, until they are made conscious by confrontations and other interventions, and can be subsequently interpreted and analyzed.

The various deceptions must be included in any list of resistances and defenses. Case histories of "deceptive types," who share certain kinds of ego, superego, self, and object relations pathology, are presented. These examples should sensitize the analyst who does not ordinarily look for or perceive deception to be alerted to its possibilities. Some of the cases presented here were treated by us many years ago, but even the most senior and experienced of analysts can be deceived. By alerting ourselves to our resistances to dealing with these issues, and to the clues presented by our patients, we find that we are better able early on in the treatment to assess a potential for deceit and to identify it once it occurs. We take early note of character anomalies and certain developmental experiences—for example, parents who were intrusive and/or deceptive—that are likely to predispose to deceptive behaviors in the developing transference.

Phenomena of dishonesty are to be found in certain transferences that can be delineated in terms of their important genetic antecedents, constellations of drive and defense, deficits in ego functioning, pathology in self and object representations, and superego pathology. Patients who deceive their analysts induce specific kinds of countertransferences, requiring special technical management on the part of the analyst. When we speak of deceptive transferences, we are abstracting out an aspect of the total transference constellation in order to focus more clearly on its deceptive component. Deceptive transferences are often found to be embedded in more "authentic" transferences and transference neuroses. In our conduct of psychoanalysis and psychotherapy, we have found that our patients shift in the transference from more mature to more primitive deceptive transference configurations, including deceptive ones.

Our case studies and vignettes demonstrate considerable ego pathology that involves dissociation of parts of the ego and the use of primitive defense mechanisms, especially projective identification. These mechanisms are central to the genesis of imposture and other forms of deception used in more limited episodic behaviors as well as those that are more extensively embedded in certain stable character formations. Significant fixations at very early, especially oral and anal levels of development are manifest in each of the cases examined. In each case, the vicissitudes of early childhood development are examined for their role in ego and superego impairment. We ask and hope to answer why some who are traumatized choose dissociative mechanisms of defense and subsequent deception, whereas others find different solutions to trauma.

In examining case histories, we learned that deceptive patients often suffered from faulty identifications with parents who lied to them or intermittently or chronically disappointed or abandoned them. Such patients often developed deceptive behaviors to deny what their parents had done, protecting them symbolically and even idealizing them, but also mocking and ridiculing them. Profound narcissistic disturbances seem to be central to the etiology of deceptive pathology. The deception serves to buttress a self experience of deficiency and powerlessness. Gottdiener (1982), for example, finds that in the background of his impostor patients, "deception, lying, and cheating were prevalent in their homes and accepted cynically as the way things were done in the world" (p. 451).

Some deceptive patients can be described as having overly harsh superego structures, with concomitant superego lacunae. The liar, for example, unconsciously seeks punishment when he lies, risks discovery of the lie, and often maintains a chronic sense of guilt over having told the lie. Guilt and its sequelae are not this evident in more extreme examples of deception, as in the case of the psychopath.

Varieties of deceptive transferences are described, and recommendations for the treatment of deceptive patients are made. The discovery of a patient's deceptions often occurs in an extra-clinical setting, as from a referral source or from a newspaper item, and the communication of the discovery to the patient requires special handling. The analyst who discovers that he or she has been deceived during the course of a session is confronted with the serious danger of countertransference enactments or counterenactments.

Recommendations are made to those analysts whose patients ask them to be deceptive themselves—to enact with the patient the parent's role, for example, as when they are asked to give false data to insurance companies.

A twice-weekly psychotherapy patient, a 40-year-old designer who came to treatment in order to understand why she had not yet succeeded in her goal of marrying and having children, reported to her analyst after ten sessions that had seemed fruitful and in which a working alliance was being established, that she had reached the limit of sessions for which her insurance company would provide reimbursement. Hereafter, she hoped that the analyst would submit claims on her mother's policy, claiming that her mother and not she herself was the patient. Furthermore, she requested that when that benefit ran out, her father would be claimed as the patient. The analyst's refusal to collude with the scheme and the invitation to explore the meaning of such a request resulted in the patient's terminating the treatment.

Several recently published studies deal with deceptive transferences. LaFarge (1994) delineates three kinds: (1) *Imposturous*, in which the patient believes his own lies, guided by a grandiose fantasy involving an inflated self-image and an identification with an idealized parent, along with a view of the analyst as a devalued object; (2) *psychopathic paranoid*, in which the patient deliberately lies, in an overt or covert attack on the analyst, while identifying alternately with the deceptive parent and the deceived child; and (3) *psychopathic unreal*, in which the patient does not believe his own lies but identifies with the parent who was experienced as dehumanized. Riesenberg-Malcolm's (1990) *as-if* analytic phenomenon refers to an inauthentic relationship in which the patient hears the analyst's interpretations, but devitalizes them in the service of keeping the status quo and blocking analytic progress. Renik (1992) writes in "Use of the Analyst as a Fetish" of a transference paradigm in which the patient does not try to understand himself but makes various uses of the relationship with the analyst instead. The patient might make attempts, for example, to seduce the analyst into doing the work for the patient, who does not think about the analysis outside the session. The analyst, then, is used by the patient and unconsciously serves often as a missing vital part, for example, the conscience. Such patients cannot or choose not themselves to function conscientiously and often lie to the analyst. Renik notes, "To themselves as well as to the analyst, some patients can lie, lie about having lied, then lie about having lied about having lied" (p. 551). Etchegoyen (1991) and Bach (1994) have conceptualized independently such transferences as "perverse": the patient treats the analyst as a thing, a part object, not a whole person. The transference perversion becomes a sexualized, repetitive undermining of the defining aspects of the psychoanalytic situation. L. Grossman (1993) notes that "neurotic defenses may be thought of as directed against wishes, whereas perverse defenses are directed against perceived reality" (p. 422). The perverse attitude defines a class of operations that involve taking certain liberties with reality. Reed (1994) has found similar transference perversions to be characterized by "pat-terned changeability" in the level of object relations. Fogel (1991) notes that the perverse paradigm is viewed by some as the"latest frontier in psychoanalysis" (p. 2), suggesting the need for an overall consciousness-raising process on the part of analysts at large.

Deception may elicit problematic countertransference reactions, some of which are induced, aroused, or brought to the surface in the analyst who feels deceived or gulled. The analyst's personal and idiosyncratic transference reactions to the deception are coupled with an alien-induced countertransference that sometimes mirrors how the patient who is deceptive must feel in his inner world. The peculiar nature of analytic work—its isolation, its detachment, its nonjudgmental quality, its libidinal aims, its "purity"—constitutes a fertile field in which analysts may become vulnerable to lies and other forms of deception. So too, does the evenly hovering stance of listening to the psychic truth of all that the patients present make for this vulnerability. Analysts are concerned primarily with the genesis of distorted perceptions while doing analytic work. They are less likely to concern themselves with the kinds of cues that others use to size up those they encounter, for they are usually not streetwise while working as analysts, even though they may be, to varying degrees, while not working analytically.

An extreme example, this time from fiction, of the analyst's dilemma is to be found in David Mamet's (1987) screenplay, *House of Games*, in which a socially isolated, overworked woman psychiatrist is fooled by the lies of a psychopathic patient and subsequently swindled by a con man. The con man challenges her threat that she will report him to the police: "And tell them what? Whatta ya gonna tell them, Stud? That a famous psychiatrist gave her cash away to some con man?" (p. 67). In his taunt, the con man indicates his awareness of important narcissistic issues such as the analyst's professional pride and wish to avoid public shame that make this form of deceit such a difficult subject for analysts to address.

Doren (1987) describes the dilemma as that between (1) disbelief with no basis for understanding or interpretation and (2) belief and "the high risk of being made to look foolish both professionally and personally," if one were to consider seriously the basis for confronting and interpreting such hurtful deceptions. Some analysts may be more vulnerable than others to lies, for the isolation of the work deprives them of and protects them from the vicissitudes of various kinds of unpleasant dealings with others.

Therefore, it is as vital for an analyst to suspend disbelief as it is to hear everything with a grain of salt. The analyst's stance is a nonjudgmental one; yet he or she should be at-the-ready to find disguise and deception. It is this paradoxical stance that makes a good analyst. In a private communication, Finkelstein (1989) has written:

> While it is likely that many analysts may be gullible and therefore vulnerable to liars, many others may react to such patients in quite another manner. One of my teachers used to say that good analysts should be a "little bit paranoid," that is, they should maintain a degree of skepticism or even suspicion about the things their patients tell them.

We begin the book with a discussion of a particularly prevalent form of deception, one for which there is no prior systematic discussion in the literature, namely patients' omissions during psychoanalytic treatment. In this discussion, we invite analysts to attend to what is not brought into the analysis and is enacted instead outside the treatment situation. Unlike the psychopath and the impostor, the omitter does not create a new, fictitious reality, but presents his reality with unexplained gaps. Omissions are multiply determined and can be understood, as can other deceptive phenomena, such as lies and imposture, from the points of view of drive theory, ego psychology, object relations theory, and self psychology. Clinical illustrations of various psychodynamic constellations are presented, and technical recommendations for treatment are offered.

> Mr. and Mrs. A., a married couple, came for marital therapy in order to resolve certain issues, such as finances and the sharing of friends. What they had failed to inform the therapist until several months after treatment had begun, was that Mr. A. was once a woman. The couple had been lesbian lovers, and one of them had had a sex-change operation.

We then progress to a discussion of gratuitous and outright lies told in treatment. Our thoughts about this subject have been stimulated by the writings of Sisela Bok (1978). In her book, *Lying: Moral Choice in Public and Private Life*, many kinds of lies are specified: black, white, and shades of gray; lying to liars and enemies; lying to protect patients and clients; lying for social science—all rationalized for the public good. Bok, a professor of ethics at Harvard, takes the moral high ground, questioning why we allow deception to be our lot. In her view, lies are like a deadly virus in a culture. She concludes, "These [deceptive] practices are not immutable. In an imperfect world, they cannot be wiped out altogether, but surely they can be reduced and counteracted. I hope to have shown how often the justifications they invoke are insubstantial and how they can disguise and fuel all other wrongs (p. 249)."

Bok is not alone in her concern about the extent of deceit inherent in our culture. In an article published in *The American Psychologist*, Saxe (1991) has quite thoughtfully remarked that

> Society cannot function well with the massive dishonesty now evident, and increasing the penalties for dishonest behavior may only serve to create additional deception. The effects of rampant dishonesty, from a lack of confidence in governmental leaders to mistrust among colleagues and friends, can only have a corrosive impact on our public and private lives. [p. 414]

He calls for a more sophisticated view of honesty and dishonesty: "The line between a lie and the truth, as psychoanalysts know, is not as clear cut as parents and an outraged public would have it" (p. 414). He points out, for example, that someone who had to be totally honest would become a social isolate.

As psychoanalysts, we need to balance Bok's position with one that, although not condoning the social and other ill effects of lying and other forms of deception, still allows room for an objective appraisal of the multiple functions that they serve and opens up possibilities for effective treatment. Daily, we work with those who hold up moral banners of compulsive honesty that veil self-punitive, masochistic, and/or sadistic agendas.

Rangell (1980), in his analysis of the public's gullibility with regard to President Nixon during the Watergate crisis, describes this "compromise of integrity":

> I was struck with a feeling of something awesome and uncanny, even, if you will believe it now, ominous and frightening, in the public's willing acceptance of the style and tone of his words; the uncritical and compliant acceptance of his artificiality, the obvious opportunism, the insincerity and the questionable credibility which comes across in his every utterance. [p. 12]

Rangell, a psychoanalyst with a social conscience and a dedication to morality and ethics, may have been among the first to have written on deception from a socioethical point of view, as well as a psychoanalytic one, which he presents with clear political bias while attempting at the same time an objective appraisal of his subject. We aim to further adumbrate the relationship between deceiver and deceived, between the impostor and the audience.

Although deception among public and famous figures is not new, we have, in recent times, been privy to facts once hidden. The credibility issues of public figures, for example, President Clinton, Colonel North, Senator Ted Kennedy, as well as of iconic figures, such as Mr. O. J. Simpson, cast some light on what goes on in the private domain, as within families. It seems entirely possible that increasing numbers of children are being raised in homes in which lies are told, and the contents of the evolving ego and superego seem to include lying as desirable, that is, as a portion of the ego-ideal. Children are developing in a world in which inauthenticity and fraudulence are in fashion, as plastic surgery, sex-change operations, and cross dressing are considered to be acceptable solutions for dealing with dysphoria. It is essential that we as psychoanalysts squarely face these issues if we are to serve the therapeutic needs of our patients in the years to come.

VARIETIES OF DECEPTION
IN THE ANALYTIC DYAD

Within the psychoanalytic encounter, a range of behaviors reflect varying degrees of authenticity, from truth to white lies to omissions to outright or "black" lies. There is a variety of deceptive character types: true impostor, psychopath, imposturous personality, false self, and as-if personality. These types of inauthenticity, though not necessarily in the order just cited, reflect a range of pathology: from ego identity synthesis and integration to fluid and fragmented identifications, from a solid sense of the reality of the self to a distorted sense of the reality of the self, and from mature to pathological object relations.

Truth

Truthful communications are those that are real, accurate, reliable, and trustworthy. However, determining what the truth is can be problematic in analytic treatment, since memory so often fails and is so often subject to distortion and other falsifications. For example, one might ask whether false recollections and screen memories are deceptive phenomena. If the answer is yes, the exclusive moral and ethical connotations we usually connect with deception of any sort must be dropped. Hanly (1990) contrasts two philosophical theories of truth: the correspondence theory, which holds that there is objectivity in perception and thought and a correspondence between an object and its description; and the coherence theory, which holds that there may be more than one description of the world. He sees the former, which allows for only one truth, as a necessary element in psychoanalysis, in addition to respect for subjectivity, relativity, and psychic reality. Bok (1978) distinguishes between truth and truthfulness: "We must single out . . . from the countless ways in which we blunder misinformed through life, that which is done with the intention to mislead and from the countless partial stabs at truth, those which are intended to be truthful" (p. 8). Bok rightly applies her judgments to the social and broader societal institutions, whereas we are considering deceptions mainly from the psychoanalytic point of view.

White Lies

White lies are untruths told to the analyst with the conscious intent of sparing pain or suffering on a personal level. Bok (1978) defines the white lie as "a falsehood not meant to injure anyone, and of little moral import" (p. 58). She wonders, though, "whether there are such lies; and if there are, whether their cumulative consequences are still without harm; and, finally, whether many lies are not defended as 'white' which are in fact harmful in their own right" (p. 58).

Usually, the white lie is intended consciously to spare the analyst some hurt that the patient unconsciously wishes for.

Gratuitous Lies

Gratuitous lies are untruths told to the analyst for no discernible conscious gain. The gratuitous lie is often about some trivial matter, and is usually told in part in order to establish psychological distance from the analyst (Lieberman 1991b). In Chapter 3, on lying, several case examples are presented in which the patient tells gratuitous lies to the analyst, which can, as Arlow (1971) notes, also relate to perversion: "The petty lie is the equivalent of the fetish—it is something which is interposed between the individual and reality in order to ward off the perception of the true reality and to substitute instead perceptions which facilitate ambiguity and illusion, both of which can be for the patient too harsh" (p. 326).

Omissions

Omissions involve the conscious or preconscious leaving out, at a particular moment or moments in the treatment, of information that would make the analyst *significantly* more knowledgeable about the patient (Lieberman 1993a,b). The withholding of this information is from the treating analyst's viewpoint unexpected, unanticipated, and completely surprising, although it might not be to an outside analyst not involved in the particular transference–countertransference dyad that such patients create. That is, the omission is surprising and at times shocking in terms of its violation of the fundamental rule of saying whatever comes to mind without prejudging its relevance and its violation of what appears to be a good working alliance. Subsequent analysis will usually reveal that the omission is consistent with the patient's unconscious motives, defenses, resistances, developmental history, and other information the analyst possesses. From the patient's viewpoint, an omission may be either conscious or unconscious. Psychoanalysis has placed extensive emphasis on the notion of omissions considered as not conscious. Preconscious censorship has been a primary focus of attention since the earliest formulations deriving from Freud's topographical model, and then later, with the development of the structural model, omissions were regarded as unconscious or preconscious functioning of the ego. The theory has not, however, accorded as much emphasis to conscious and deliberate omissions. We understand the unconscious deception that serves multiple functions quite differently from the way we understand and treat conscious deceptions that take the form of omissions.

Secrets

Secrets are special subtypes of omissions, consciously withheld from the analyst. Greenson (1967) and Ekstein and Caruth (1972) write that secrets are a way of dealing with fantasies involving shame. We subsume such secrets under the category of omissions. We instead define a secret in the analytic encounter as something chronically concealed from the analyst; the patient rationalizes that its revelation to the analyst will be tantamount to a betrayal of some outside person, persons, or group. Examples of such secrets, the telling of which is often avoided in treatment, are stock market information, government information, or confidences told to patient by people the analyst knows. The keeping of such secrets carries with it not just unconscious gratifications of an unspecified nature but also the further resistance potential of the insidious spreading out and of adhesiveness of the secret itself to other related information.

Outright Lies

Outright lies, colloquially called black lies, are those that are told consciously and deliberately to the analyst about something of importance, in order to mislead him or her. Fenichel (1939) defines the lie as "an untruth in which the subject himself did intend to deceive others with his assertions and did not believe the assertions himself" (pp. 130–131). Kursh (1971) defines the lie as "not just a false statement; it is a special class of false statement . . . deliberately provided to mislead the steps of the unwary, to turn them in a direction that will for one reason or another benefit the speaker" (p. 192).

OTHER RELATED DECEPTIVE PHENOMENA

"Pseudologia Fantastica"

Deutsch (1923) and Fenichel (1939) refer to *pseudologia fantastica* as the creation of elaborate fantasies that serve the defensive function of denial and disavowal, which are then actually believed to be true by the patient. The patient, classically diagnosed as hysterical, gets carried away by what was initially recognized as a falsification and, as he or she elaborates, comes to believe in the veracity of the escalated fantastic elaborations. He or she then brings in other material that substantiates the fantasies, which often reach grossly mythological proportions. Additionally, the patient attempts to make the analyst a witness by getting him or her to believe in the truth of the fantasy. Some aspect of the real truth is always embedded in the fantasy, as is also the case with screen memories, to be discussed below. This relationship of real truth to fantasy brings us into the area of psychic reality, for no matter how much deception psychic reality may contain, there is always a form of psychic truth to be reckoned with, in keeping with Hanly's (1990) "correspondence theory" and Freud's views of objective truth and material reality having an impact on psychic reality.

Screen Memories

These are fragmented memories of the long forgotten years of childhood that return as a defensive cover for other, usually earlier but sometimes later, associated but repressed memories. They themselves may be true, false, or a mixture. They usually involve a degree of wish fulfillment, but also involve disguise, as do all compromise formations. That is, memories that date from earlier or later experiences contain falsification and deception that disguise a truth, as the individuals who employ such memories use partial or relatively benign truths to conceal less acceptable, more threatening truths connected with events from another point in time.

Personal Myth

The personal myth (Kris 1956), like screen memories and distorted autobiographical memories, involves the falsification of memory, which relates, in this instance, to a crucial part of the patient's idealized self-image. By the combined selection and exclusion of memory, the myth of the idealized self often contains and/or relates to a repressed *family romance fantasy*, another relevant form of deception involving narcissistic needs, which shores up the value of the parents. They become represented in idealized, false parental imagoes, such as kings and queens.

Illusion

Illusion makes use of denial of painful reality and of wish fulfillment, so that an improbable but possible event is expected and anticipated. The event is improbable, but could occur, and is to be distinguished from delusion in that there is a higher degree of reality testing: the chances of fulfilling the wish are within the range of possible if not probable expectation.

Delusion

Delusion is a distorted and false sense organ perception that involves impaired reality testing, clearly contradicting what is and what is not possible.

False Memory and False Memory Syndrome (FMS)

FMS is a condition in which the patient's identity and relationships are centered around the memory of an objectively false traumatic experience, but the patient strongly believes it to be true. Often, as has occurred recently, these false memories of trauma result from "brain washing" by some individual or agency whose personal interests are served if the memory is confessed. FMS has a devastating effect on the patient and typically produces a continuing dependency on the police, therapist, or therapeutic program that iatrogenically created the syndrome. Typical are the induced memories that one has been abducted by extraterrestial agents, or that one has committed or been the victim of satanic cult incest and rape that never in fact have occurred.

Malingering

Malingering involves the voluntary production and presentation of false or grossly exaggerated physical or psychological symptoms. Such falsification is done with some specific goal in mind, such as to avoid work or the draft or to be compensated for employment disabilities.

Munchausen Syndrome

This factitious disorder is similar to malingering, but there is no recognizable goal of monetary profit and compensation. The important motive is the deception of and psychological involvement with the doctor whom the liar wishes to impress and endear. In the Munchausen by Proxy Syndrome (MBPS), a mother exaggerates or lies to the doctor about a fatal ailment suffered by her infant, thereby using her infant child to create a relationship with the doctor in which lying is the mode of interaction. Instead of following the physician's advice to heal the child, the mother often deliberately places her child in jeopardy, exacerbating the symptoms. The infant, who is often murdered by the mother's grossly mishandled medical ministrations, which she engages in for purposes of her wishful libidinal and narcissistic relationship with her child's physician, is therefore used as a fetish, or an object for the barter of affections. Schreier's (1992) and Schreier and Libow's (1993) recent work in this area emphasize the various lies the mother tells the physician about how good a mother she is. The physician, like so many others in dyads of deception, believes the lies in efforts to be a good doctor despite evidence that could easily dispel them if not for misplaced good faith in the doctoring interaction.

DECEPTIVE CHARACTER TYPES FOUND IN PSYCHOANALYTIC TREATMENT

Impostors

The impostor passes himself off incognito in a psychopathic way, as possessing an identity of someone other than himself, and is convincing about it, not immediately inspiring doubt in the other. According to Gediman (1985a), an impostor is one "who assumes an identity or a title not his own." In psychoanalysis, the *true* impostor, one who misrepresents himself, has been the subject of a few studies; notably by Abraham (1925), Deutsch (1955), Greenacre (1958a,b), and Kaplan (1989). Typically such an individual suffers from a severe character disorder; he or she engages in delinquent, psychopathic, and sociopathic acts or other criminal behavior with the conscious and deliberate intention to deceive in ways facilitated by his false identity.

Imposturous Tendencies

Short of being a true impostor, individuals may exhibit a range of imposturous tendencies. According to Gediman (1985a), imposturous tendencies ranging from the least to the most pathological occur in a wide variety of personality disturbances and situations. At the least pathological end is the promotion of illusion and disguise within the bounds of creative art and play. At the more pathological end of the nosological spectrum would be borderline personalities with as-if tendencies. We present a series of such character types in Chapter 4 on imposture, and in Chapter 5 we discuss issues posed by imposturous supervisees.

Those Who Wrongly Believe They Are Impostors

In this category are those who experience themselves and their achievements as inauthentic, fake, and fraudulent, but who in reality have been productive or accomplished. Greenacre (1958b) cites the case of Fritz Kreisler, who felt inauthentic presenting his own composed music as his own work and attributed authorship of his original works to older male composers. He was an impostor in reverse, a different but related category that is also typified by very successful, high-powered women who have suddenly come into new managerial and leadership roles, previously assumed mainly by men, and cannot quite shake the feeling of being fraudulent. Social factors contribute to their difficulties in stepping into bigger shoes; underlying dynamics often involve castration wishes, penis envy, and fear of object loss if they are more accomplished than their mates.

False Self

This is a term used by Winnicott (1960), who describes a form of nonexistence

> where the True Self is split off from and hidden by the False Self, in attempts to conform to parental expectations which are derailed from any empathic understanding of the child's true developmental potential. Such individuals often have a poor capacity for using symbols and are impoverished with respect to developing cultural and creative values. Instead of cultural pursuits, such persons exhibit extreme restlessness, an inability to concentrate, and a need to collect impingements from external reality so that the living time of the individual can be filled by reactions to these impingements. [p. 150]

Such individuals lead lives filled with those reactions, rather than with self-initiated activities, or what Winnicott regarded as a more productive form of existence.

As-If Personalities

As-if pathology is characterized by a disturbance in identity. As described by Deutsch (1942) and Ross (1967), individuals with this disturbance are prone to mimicry and unstable, shifting, unintegrated, superficial identifications, based on a lack of stability in the earliest object relations, where there has been insufficient differentiation from the object. While the true impostor pretends under the literal cover of someone else's name, the as-if personality, lacking a cohesive, stable, integrated identification, unconsciously takes on the color and style of admired individals through mimicry and imitation. A subtype of the as-if personality might be called "shifty characters." These patients show a lack of forthrightness and directness about who they are and what they do, and they instigate the analyst to doubt them. They lack integrity and do not back up what they say with actions.

> John thought of himself as a possible fraud and phony, yet did well in his work. When his bill payment was due, he would tell his analyst that he would bring in a check the next time or send one in the mail. This went on for weeks until the analyst suspected that he had conflicting, shifting intentions and was never sure whether he would pay or not, was lying, or never intended to pay. Then John sent the check, canceling out the fantasy he had instigated himself.

Psychopathic Characters

Psychopathic characters behave toward others and their possessions in a manner that indicates severe superego pathology, that is, a lack of internalization of the ethical standards of society and of guilt or remorse for wrongdoing. According to Meloy (1988), the psychopath gets his victim, who may be the therapist, to identify with him or her in a process he terms "malignant pseudo-identification." He speaks of the vulnerability of those who are in the helping professions to the psychopath's "affective simulation," denying their own needs and perceiving themselves as altruists. This is consistent with the point we made earlier in connection with Mamet's (1987) fictionalized con man who fooled his psychiatrist by exploiting her professional pride.

SUMMARY

In the chapters that follow, we aim to demonstrate and discuss some of the varieties of deception and deceptive transferences we have encountered clinically in conducting psychoanalytic and psychotherapeutic work and have learned about from our students in supervision.

We emphasize the role of sadomasochistic fantasy in these transferences, which pervert and subvert the central task of the analytic work, which is to search for the genetic antecedents of the patient's presenting problems, the unconscious core conflicts, and fantasies. Patients who manifest such transferences are predominantly orally and anally fixated, the sadistic components of these fixations resulting in a mocking of and contempt for the analyst and the treatment. They attack and assault the analyst's sense of reality through the lie and through the use of projective identification. In these patients, ego pathology is characterized by dissociation and fragmentation, the failure of internalization, identity diffusion, and weak boundaries that enable them to use projective identification as a defense. There are narcissistic disturbances—low self-esteem oscillates with grandiosity as the analyst is alternately devalued and idealized. The primary identifications often have been with parents who have been deceptive themselves.

The superego development of these patients has been sporadic. Overly harsh superego fragments and broad lacunae coexist along with severe guilt and acting out in punishment-seeking ways. There has been a lack of prohibition against deceit, from parents and society at large.

Additionally, we have found that those who deceive their analysts have had mothers who could not attune to them or be with them in consistent ways. Many were sent away to relatives as infants for periods of time; others had a history of multiple caretakers. Inconsistencies and gaps in their communications were not noted by others. Similarly, Bach's (1994) perverse patients are described as perceiving "gaps" in their mothers that seem to him to be more than just fantasies based on perceptions of the mothers' genitals. They react and respond to the gaps in the relatedness of the mothers.

Deception and the deceptive transferences must be analyzed in order for treatment to begin in an authentic way. In addition to the classic points of view involving drive, defense, and object, we also agree with Bion (1970), who sees the deceptive dyad as one between parasite and host. He views it as destructive to both, unconsciously designed to destroy both participants:

In psychoanalysis, the liar is a significant fact and gains significance from the lying nature of what he says. The parasitic relationship between liar and environment, corresponding to the parasitic relationship between the thinker and the lie, denudes the environment of significance. The analyst who accepts such lies is acting as host; if he does not he contributes to the feeling of persecution by "being" an unthought thought, a thought without a thinker. [p. 104]

Part I

IN THE
ANALYTIC
ENCOUNTER

2

OMISSIONS
IN PSYCHOANALYTIC
TREATMENT

In this chapter we examine and elucidate a common obstacle to the conduct of psychoanalytic treatment, that of the patient's omissions. Omissions are ubiquitous. Nevertheless, some patients select from the universe of possibilities for free association what *is needed* for the analyst to understand and to analyze them. Others select, consciously and unconsciously, just so the analyst will *not* really understand them.

An experienced analyst expects certain omissions. For example, in the early phases of treatment, many patients are reluctant to talk about emerging transference reactions or about specific subjects or incidents they are ashamed to reveal, such as rejections, abortions, and homosexual feelings. Our focus, however, is on omissions that are unexpected and unanticipated, carry with them an element of surprise, and fall into the category of the deceptive and not the average expectable, as in resistances

Note: This chapter is based on two papers presented by Dr. Lieberman. The first, "What Is Missing in this Picture" was presented at the meeting of Division 39 of the American Psychological Association, New York City, April 1993. The second, "Omissions in Psychoanalytic Treatment," was presented at the 38th Congress of the International Psychoanalytic Association, Amsterdam, July, 1993.

motivated by shame and guilt. Riviere (1936), in her discussion of the manic defenses of those with negative therapeutic reactions, notes that "certain patients of this type especially withhold from us all 'evidence' of an indisputable character in support of our interpretations. There are degrees to which this resistance can completely defeat an analytic endeavor" (p. 419). Unexplained latenesses, cancellations, no-shows, or sudden vacations may signal the possibility of omissions.

As beginning psychoanalysts, we were instructed to attend to and to analyze as fully as possible our patients' associations, memories, fantasies, and dreams and to attend to what they *leave out* in their communications to us. We were privileged to have Freud's brilliant mind as a role model and to be able to follow its intricate workings as his thoughts and analytic acumen turned to the various meanings of the myriad gaps and omissions in the associations of the obsessional Rat Man (1909). Freud alerted us to the significance of unconscious omissions, but did not deal sufficiently with omissions that were quite conscious and intentional. In present-day practice, we are accustomed, as part of our legacy from the early days, to working more with what is brought in and acted in, than with what is not brought in and acted out.

The idea that patients consciously and deliberately omit significant material can make analysts uncomfortable. Analysts at times are overly dependent upon or take too much solace from certain assumptions, for example, (1) all will eventually emerge in the transference, (2) there are often periods of time in every analysis when the material is chaotic and not yet understandable, and (3) all events that are dynamically central at a particular time will be reported honestly and around that time. We challenge the usefulness of these assumptions in the treatment of certain patients who are prone to deception.

The psychoanalytic literature "omits" the topic of conscious omissions with but a few exceptions. Fenichel (1939) considers omissions as "negative lies" and stresses the obsessional's tendency to omit. Kris (1956), in his paper on the personal myth, writes about the way in which certain individuals use exaggeratedly positive autobiographical memories as a protective screen against painful experiences, with the benign outline and rich details of their mythic creations covering over significant omissions and distortions. "Only after omissions have been filled in and distortions have been corrected, can access to the repressed material be gained" (p. 653).

Sandler and Sandler (1987) allot conscious and preconscious omissions a central place in their schema contrasting the present unconscious with the past unconscious. The concept of the present unconscious holds that omissions are inevitable ways of avoiding shame or feeling silly—all of the feelings that the patient consciously wants to avoid in the analytic situation and that enter into conscious censorship of embarrassing thoughts and feelings. They emphasize the importance of what Freud, in his early topographical model of the mind, called the "second censorship," or the more superficial censor between the system's conscious (Cs.) and preconscious (Pcs.) This more conscious censorship, serving the narcissistic resistances, protects the patient from feeling silly or ashamed were he or she to speak to the analyst about painful matters that have not gotten so far as to be dynamically repressed. These repressed matters, with which analysts are more accustomed to dealing, are usually subject to the more powerful censorship between the preconscious (Pcs.) and the unconscious (Ucs.) and strictly speaking do not correspond to what we mean when we speak of conscious omissions that constitute only temporarily "forgotten" and not dynamically repressed material in the analytic session: "It reflects primarily the difference that existed in childhood between that which could be carried on in secret and that which could be allowed to be seen by others" (Sandler and Sandler 1987, pp. 336–337).

Sandler and Sandler specifically allude to

what the patient is conscious of but does not report to the analyst. . . . There is a tendency in psychoanalytic writing and discussion to minimize the significance of this level of functioning and to assume that the patient's overt associations are entirely allusions to *unconscious* fantasies and feelings on the part of the patient. Yet we all know that they can just as much reflect thoughts, fantasies, and feelings *that are conscious but not expressed*. [p. 334]

References to actions, present, past, and intended for the future, should be added to this list.

At the onset of treatment, often in the initial interview, some patients present their life histories in such a way that the analyst has a full view of who they are. Others present just a slice of life, and the analyst is often left to infer what has not been presented or is put into the position of having to ask a question about why something in particular has not been mentioned. This is, of course, a standard technique of resistance analysis that is equally applicable to the analysis of omissions. Patients then may feel that free association is no longer free, and the matter becomes complicated with the fantasy that they are being put on the spot, influenced, and coerced. The analyst's neutrality becomes compromised by the selectivity involved in asking the question. Some patients are aware of the kinds of information the analyst needs to know in order to help them. They are often referred to as gifted analysands. Others are more involved in a selective process of impression management. Still other patients may assume and fantasize, consciously or unconsciously, that their analysts are omnipotent and omniscient, and know everything regardless of whether or not they put their ideas into words. Others experience the analyst internally as a parent who decathected them and did not need to know or care to know. Some withhold in order to protect themselves from the analyst as an intrusive parent. Omissions thus have a myriad of meanings with respect to object relations and transference.

A patient who omits reporting important life events—for example, his discovery at age 18 that he was adopted—or who omits something extraordinary that happened the very morning before a session—for example, his having had intercourse with his ex-girlfriend whom the analyst thought was out of his life—often seems unaware of the deleterious effect the omissions could have on the treatment. That is to say, the omissions interfere with and seriously stifle the potential therapeutic impact of the myriad connections the analyst could otherwise be making, as, for example, between affects that appear incomprehensible and the events that triggered them and that would make them comprehensible in context. These patients need help, have entered treatment ostensibly to receive it, but cannot or will not communicate to their analysts what they need to know. That patients render their analysts helpless to help them is a naggingly familiar problem and one that takes on special meaning in the case of deception by omission.

Omissions can be confused easily with certain mechanisms of defense, particularly repression, suppression, dissociation, and splitting, all of which serve as resistance. Yet, omissions seem to merit a category of their own. What is selected via conscious and unconscious choices spans a range of clinical pictures that are full or narrow band with respect to the normality or pathology of the process of omitting and the content of the omissions. Examples of how one judges the significance of material that is left out is presented below.

Freud's (1937) instruction that the analyst take a neutral attitude and listen with evenly hovering attention leads us to assume that *all* relevant material will eventually appear and that our patients will cooperate in a corresponding manner by free associating and providing us with all the necessary pieces we need to work with. As a way of encouraging us, Freud wrote in *Constructions in Analysis* (1937) that the analyst works under more favorable conditions than the archaeologist. For his task of reconstruction, "all of the essentials are preserved, even things that are completely forgotten are present somehow and somewhere, and have been buried and made inaccessible to the subject" (p. 276). One year later, however, in *Splitting of the Ego in the Process of Defense* (1938), Freud presents another point of view: "The synthetic function of the ego, though it is of such extraordinary importance, is subject to particular conditions and is liable to a whole series of disturbances" (p. 221). He was acknowledging the advances of ego psychology in understanding the variations in functioning of a broader range of latter-day patients who could not be expected to be as amenable to the classic treatment approaches. Freud did not shrink from asking numerous questions of his patients. Looking back, this could have been his effort to counteract the effects of the character pathology underlying conscious deception. Modern trends toward less active questioning could encourage more omissions and gaps than Freud's more actively vigilant stance. The work of Poland (1985) is a welcome addition in its advocacy of an active analytic stance needed to pursue the possibilities of omission.

Omissions raise important issues about ego structure and ego strength, and about superego structure and superego strength, which bear significantly on technique. Kernberg (1992) speaks of transferences of dishonest communication and issues of character. "To tell the truth, the whole truth, and nothing but the truth" is an implicit maxim for both members of the analytic dyad, and both understand that the truth is slow in emerging. Patients are instructed to say whatever comes to mind and not to censor. For some, particularly those prone to deception, the trust that is involved in following the fundamental rule of free association and of establishing a good working alliance is difficult to achieve. Analysts disagree about whether patients should or should not be urged to tell everything on their minds, thereby following the basic rule. They weigh the benefits of having a seemingly good working alliance against the patient's experiencing the analytic situation as a confessional or courtroom, with the analyst as intrusive, judgmental, or punitive and the analysis as one more time and place in their lives in which their autonomy is threatened. Yet, the working alliance is compromised if omissions are overlooked. Such transferential reactions are to be analyzed rather than to be avoided and counteracted in ways that analysts sometimes falsely presume would preserve autonomy and freedom.

Omissions in everyday social relationships can be adaptive, and being selective about what one imparts to others can be regarded as a sign of maturity. This is not so in the analytic situation. Omissions are a form of deception, of selective reporting, similar to but different from lies. A lie told to the analyst, as defined in Chapter 1, is an untruth told consciously with an intent to deceive (Blum 1983, Fenichel 1939, Gediman 1985a,b, Lieberman 1991b, Weinshel 1979). A piece of reality is consciously distorted or invented: a lie is an act of *commission*. An omission, on the other hand, distorts reality by leaving a gap, but it does not create a fictitious reality. It reveals something about the drives: perhaps a wish to rebel against following the fundamental rule. As was just stated, it also reveals something about the superego, perhaps a character defect around issues of honesty. And the omission reveals something about the patient's object relations, such as ambivalence and a wish to devalue the person consulted for help. Finally, it says something about the patient's narcissistic balance, perhaps that omissions restore the self-esteem that is damaged by having to reveal while the analyst is permitted to conceal. Conscious omissions of material that later is brought into the analysis are eventually analyzable in most cases. That is, the emergent material often reveals analyzable motives to distort reality, to avoid pain, to achieve pleasure, to express aggression, to maintain narcissistic balance, and to hold onto the object, as well as many other motivations that are to be explored throughout this book.

CLINICAL ILLUSTRATIONS

Several brief clinical illustrations and then two more detailed reports clarify what is meant by a *significant* omission, the failure to reveal material that could be of importance to the analyst in his or her effort to understand the patient. In some instances, the patients themselves acknowledged having omitted something significant at an earlier date. More often, the analysts came upon

the omissions themselves, either in some extra-analytic situation, such as from information provided by the referral source,
or by sensitively detecting that something had been left out in
the patient's associations. Analysts will recognize many of these
omissions as illustrative of the psychopathology of everyday life
and of everyday clinical practice.

Although ubiquitous and, in that sense, normative, omissions
are seldom focused upon in the literature as material to be analyzed. With the general advancement of analytic technique and
with growing wisdom among analysts accruing from their shared
experiences, we observe now a less naive attitude toward garden-
variety omissions. As a mark of general progress, we no longer
assume that even the most analyzable patients are capable at all
times of following the basic rule and free associating. Even the
best of analysands omit critical material. Furthermore, we no
longer assume that the only omissions that occur are due to
unconscious resistances and never to conscious intentions to
withhold, even though we respect and try to understand whatever unconscious meaning that conscious withholding may have
for the patient.

• Mr. A. spent an inordinate amount of time in his three-
times-a-week treatment complaining of his wife's selfishness and
stinginess. He never once reported what the analyst had initially
learned from the referring analyst who was treating his wife—
that his wife was paying for his treatment!

• Mrs. B., a writer who came to treatment for help in over-
coming a work inhibition, reported only when she entered the
third year of her four-times-a-week analysis that she got "stoned"
on marijuana every night, belatedly shedding some light on her
foggy state of mind during a number of sessions and finally illuminating one source of her symptom.

• Mr. C. was in a very successful three-times-weekly psychoanalytic therapy in which many painful issues had been worked
through and a strong working alliance had been established early.
He had spoken freely about all kinds of matters and early on had

reported taking his younger sister's dolls when he was an ado-
lescent and "raping" them. It was not until late in his treatment
that he reported what he had withheld—the unrepressed information that he had *actually had* sexual relations with his sister.

• Mr. D., an obsessional neurotic, was in a satisfactory four-
times-a-week psychoanalysis for four years. His analyst found
himself walking behind him in the street after a session had
ended. He saw Mr. D. taking four steps and a hop, four steps
and a hop, for several blocks. This compulsive behavior had
never been reported.

• Mr. E., after three years of twice-weekly therapy, reported
that every evening after work he lapsed into a foglike depression and expressed his anger at his analyst for never dealing with
it, even though he had never mentioned it. A symbiotic fantasy
about the analyst's omniscience was operative.

• Miss F. reported making many "hang-up" calls to her lover
to determine the latter's whereabouts and to see if she could detect secrets about his life. She did not tell her analyst that she
also called her, but the analyst suspected that the "hang-up" calls
she received around the time that the patient told her of making
the others must be coming from the patient. Perhaps the patient
was signaling her to analyze the omission in the transference in
this particular way.

It is apparent from these vignettes that the analysts' overall
listening would have been keener and better focused had they
known what was left out.

Two cases of some greater length in which omissions ham-
pered the progress of the treatment are now presented. One treatment was successful, and the other, as it eventually turned out,
was not so successful.

Miss Atlas, a 24-year-old, bright, attractive art student, the
daughter of a high-school teacher and an extremely successful
advertising agency executive, was referred for psychoanalytic
psychotherapy. She found herself unable to make a real com-

mitment to her boyfriend or to her work, and she constantly wondered whether another career would suit her better. She also found herself unable to concentrate. Although she was quite talented in several artistic arenas, she would stop short of completing any project, just when the possibility of success loomed before her. Her family had moved a number of times when she was a child, and she had had multiple caretakers, including her mother, nannies, private counselors, and the staffs in various boarding schools. Miss Atlas's parents managed to keep their tormented marriage together by being apart. Father was usually away traveling for business.

From early adolescence on, Miss Atlas was exposed by both parents to tales of their sex life and her father's affairs. She was coerced by her mother to play detective, ferreting out information about her father's many paramours. Both parents seemed to demonstrate considerable ego and superego pathology. Father's self-made success, his tremendous wealth, and his widely publicized acclaim made it difficult for Miss Atlas to de-idealize him. To complicate matters further, he performed a mothering function for her, for when he was home he was always pleasant and nurturant. What in most families was kept secret and private was not in her family. On the other hand, both parents harbored myriad secrets, lies, and omissions.

During the first two years of Miss Atlas's treatment, considerable progress was made in her ability to focus and concentrate, in asserting herself with her boyfriend, and in making some career decisions that led to her exhibiting her work in the professional arena. She no longer played detective for her mother and refused to listen to her stories about her father's sex life. She worked analytically, bringing in dreams and memories and weaving her associations from past to present. She would not, however, come more than twice a week, although she reported that she found the treatment to be quite gratifying. Considerable analysis of her fantasies and conflicts about deeper commitment did not change her refusal to increase the frequency of sessions.

In addition, from time to time she did not come and did not call, leaving her analyst perplexed and unable to discern any consistent patterns in the sessions prior to her absences that could explain such behavior. Her analyst's countertransference at these times consisted of transitory feelings of intense pain and anxiety about whether her patient would ever return to treatment, feelings induced by Miss Atlas. When she did return, Miss Atlas could not remember why she did not come to sessions. She seemed to be withholding consciously at those times. The analyst treated this behavior as something to understand. It became apparent that Miss Atlas was repeating with her analyst a reversal of her experience of her father's many absences when she was a child. Neither his arrivals nor his departures were ever announced. She learned defensively not to care about his absences and not to wonder where he was. When her father was away, her mother was depressed and angry and did not give the children basic care, so it was as if both parents were lost.

During the next two years, careful attention to the issue of Miss Atlas's absences revealed that she was extraordinarily depressed when she did not come to her sessions. She never mentioned these depressed affects in her associations. She only later disclosed that she had what she called "a little affair" on those days, eventually understood as enactments of an identification with her adulterous father. She also omitted speaking about several bulimic episodes in which she would take in vast quantities of food, representing the intrusive maternal introject, and then vomit it out. Her not coming to sessions represented, both consciously and unconsciously, her wish to keep the analyst out. Had the analyst not suspected that the absences represented resistances to talking about transferences, and had she not inquired as to what was going on on the days of the missed sessions, this important material would most probably never have come up.

Further analysis of Miss Atlas's omissions led to the emergence of a fantasy, heretofore unconscious, that she had a hidden penis that would enable her to win anything she would compete for.

The anxieties about winning and the repression of the fantasy led to her stopping short of success in her work. On the one occasion that she used the bathroom down the hall from the analyst's office in midsession, she returned reporting that she had had the fantasy that the analyst was envious of her, perhaps because of her father's wealth. She then reported the following dream: "Part of my leg was a prosthesis—a plastic part. I don't know if I could take it off or felt it as part of my leg. A woman or a man looked at it and said, 'You're suffering from misogyny.' None of what I was suffering from was clear in the dream." Her associations were to the demeaning roles that women are forced to play in society. She spoke of considerable feelings of shame. She felt that she was weird, different from others, and had felt that way since she was a child. She experienced tremendous shame over having lost urinary and bowel control when she was 4 years old, at the time her family moved. As an adult, any rejection or physical illness became associated with feeling dirty and disgusting.

After her longest disappearance from treatment, lasting four weeks, she returned unannounced, and found the analyst waiting for her at the regular time of her hour. She acknowledged her disappearance for the first time. Up until that time she always seemed to have forgotten that she had missed sessions and left it up to the analyst to remind her. She vehemently declared that she hated the analyst and wanted to hurt her as she had been hurt by her father's absences. She recalled that, when he was away, she was left alone with her mother. Her mother, at these times, would psychologically "disappear" into her own shell. When Father was home and she attempted to attract his attention she also felt she was bad, as if Mother saw her as one of Father's girlfriends and hated her for it. It is clear that narcissistic trauma was involved at each of the psychosexual phases of her development.

Miss Atlas manifested considerable ego pathology in certain areas, as in anticipation and planning. She did not have at hand certain basic information, such as travel directions and geo-

graphical facts. Many facts and memories were stored in fragments. Over time, this pathology began to improve. The treatment proved to be successful, in part because of the assiduous
attention to and analysis of the repressed material covered over
by the omissions.

Mrs. Bernstein, an extremely beautiful and bright 30-year-old
woman, was the youngest of three daughters of a wealthy
divorced couple. Like Miss Atlas, she was raised by a series of
nannies, several of whom were not English-speaking and, also
like Miss Atlas, was subjected to a constant change of boarding
schools. She reported being "dumped" in a New England boarding school at the age of 9 so that her mother could "husband-
hunt." She came to treatment in order to resolve an unhappy
relationship with a man and to obtain some career direction. She
had not worked in two years.

She had had four previous analysts, all of whom were somewhat known to her current analyst by reputation. She came for
a four-times-weekly analysis during which it eventually emerged
that she had a hidden agenda to prove herself sane and competent and to refute the ominous prognostic assessment made by
the previous analysts. In many ways she appeared to have good
potential as an analysand: her perceptiveness, excellent memory,
orderliness, capacity to free associate as well as to regularly attend
sessions, and ability to connect material from one session to the
next were all encouraging signs. Furthermore, she discarded the
antidepressants her most recent analyst had prescribed, with no
apparent effect on her mood state, so at the beginning, her new
analyst assessed her ego functioning as strong, despite her history. The analyst hypothesized that her problems were most
probably due to unresolved intrapsychic conflicts involving such
issues as latent homosexuality and oedipal fixation. Mrs.
Bernstein was reluctant to use the couch, but did so. Although
her analyst was aware of feeling competitive with the four previous analysts, she felt confident about her assessment of Mrs.
Bernstein as neurotic. The patient attributed her career stagna-

tion to her not having to earn a living and, more importantly, to her reluctance to give up her daily socializing with two friends who served as mother figures and with whom she shopped, had lunch, and played tennis.

Over the next three years, her analyst began to detect more serious pathology. The word "detect" is used because Mrs. Bernstein did not wish to view some of the symptoms that she offhandedly mentioned as having even remote psychological meaning and was vigilant that there be no such allegation. It became increasingly apparent that, although Mrs. Bernstein never stated it explicitly, she led an incredibly restricted life, circulating in a four-square block area around her apartment and walking only somewhat further to come to treatment.

It was not until the third year of treatment that she made any mention of her essential agoraphobia, her fear of touching strangers, or her fear of sitting where they had sat in a public bus—these were major omissions. These symptoms were ego-syntonic and did not just emerge as therapeutic regressions during the analysis. She seemed to be suffering from a severe narcissistic and paranoid disorder. It was necessary to analyze the omissions for the work to go forward, but also to proceed very carefully due to the nature of Mrs. Bernstein's pathology.

Mrs. Bernstein's associations were filled with allusions to a number of famous close friends, many of whom were written about in the media. The analyst learned from a television newscast that the woman Mrs. Bernstein claimed to be her best friend had married, and noted to herself that Mrs. Bernstein had not mentioned being invited to the wedding or even, for that matter, that there was to be a wedding. The analyst gently mentioned having seen the event reported, and Mrs. Bernstein anxiously shifted away from the topic. The analyst chose not to question her more thoroughly because of her considerable narcissistic vulnerability. The omission seemed related to her envy of her "best friend," as well as to the probability that this woman viewed Mrs. Bernstein only as an acquaintance, which was experienced as a deep hurt and humiliation.

After some analysis of Mrs. Bernstein's fear of contamination in public places, related to her fantasy of the maternal introject as poisonous and its subsequent projection, she began to venture out of her house more often. She attended courses that would enable her to enter a profession and required her to travel by public bus. She enjoyed her classes, but began to have disagreements with her female professor, for whom she had contempt. This behavior was understood by the analyst to reflect a split in the previously all-idealizing transference. Mrs. Bernstein then reported tearfully that she went by public bus to a dangerous and remote part of the city in order to have a dress form made. It was unclear just what this meant to her, but perhaps it had to do with some problems centered on the consolidation of body boundaries. Then by chance, the analyst read in the recent issue of a popular journal that a famous beauty, who had married one of Mrs. Bernstein's alleged former boyfriends, had had a dress form made to her measure. Mrs. Bernstein never mentioned this stimulus to her journey, with its possible homosexual and oedipal competitive meanings. Mrs. Bernstein's oldest sister was an actress. She hardly ever mentioned her sister. She had psychically sliced this sister out of her life. One week, seemingly out of the blue, she spoke of her jealousy of and rage at her sister. She never mentioned what her analyst had already learned—that her sister had that week received favorable reviews for a part she played in a Broadway show.

Both consciously and unconsciously, Mrs. Bernstein omitted in her associations information that would have led to a more thorough analysis of her conflicts. Her early childhood experiences were such that her ego was split: that is, affective experiences that were uncomfortable and hurtful were internally represented as separate from the objects that caused them. In this way, she could preserve her objects as idealized. Mrs. Bernstein's high social status and attempts at aggrandizing the status of famous people were insufficient to defend her inner self from the feelings of shame and inferiority that she had continually disowned. Treatment ended with some gains, but was incomplete because of the impasse over the amount of material withheld. The analyst felt that she could not be confronted, that she was too fragile. Attempts to deal with her omissions led consistently to severe regressive episodes. Mrs. Bernstein came to treatment ultimately to obtain reassurance that she was not damaged and then withheld in a selective manner in order to present a case for this reassurance. She could not admit that she experienced any sense of damage and became upset if such a possibility was alluded to.

What was learned from the difficulties in analyzing omissions in this case was useful in evaluating and understanding similar difficulties in treating several narcissistic patients seen over many years who came to treatment with similar hidden agendas. Early in treatment, usually after three or four sessions, they reported great gains and broadcasted their analyst's talents to their friends and relatives. They thus avoided deeper engagement in the treatment and any substantial investigation of their difficulties. They reported contentment with the treatment, told their friends they had "graduated," and seemed hurt by the analysts' diplomatic statements that they were perplexed because they did not know them very well. In retrospect, these patients clearly were quintessential omitters.

DISCUSSION

The cases of Miss Atlas and Mrs. Bernstein as well as the brief vignettes cited demonstrate the defensive function of omissions in patients who initially seemed more intact and integrated in ego structure than proved to be the case. Anna Freud (1946) alerts us to the ego's myriad ways of defeating treatment: "We are all familiar with the accusation not infrequently made against analysts—that they may have a good knowledge of a patient's unconscious, but are bad judges of his ego. There is a certain amount of justification in this criterion, for the analyst lacks

opportunities of observing the patient's whole ego in action"
(p. 23). She goes on to write:

> The ego is antagonistic to the analysis, in that it is unreliable and
> biased in its self-observation and, while conscientiously register-
> ing and passing on certain facts, falsifies and rejects others and
> prevents them from coming to light, a procedure wholly contrary
> to the methods of analytic research, which insists on seeing every-
> thing that emerges without discrimination. [pp. 31–32]

Schafer (1968) also writes of the variety of ways the ego's
synthetic function could operate:

> What has failed to be synthesized, or what has been denied syn-
> thesis, may range all the way from superficial ideas that are con-
> tradictory or unconditional to major competing suborganizations
> of the personality. . . . Through the exercise of logic and objec-
> tive judgment, the subject may choose from among competing
> ideas the one that fits best into existing organizations of ideas,
> and he may reject those that contradict or create tension in these
> organizations. This is the work of exclusion. [p. 98]

Schafer's "exclusions" refer to aspects of self-integration, and
although they are quite different from what are here called omissions, they are theoretically continuous with them, and can provide us with further insight into the nature of the ego functioning of certain patients. To understand better the phenomena of
ego- and self-integration, we can keep in mind some of the following questions as the analytic work proceeds.

- To what extent are a particular patient's omissions a function of defenses such as splitting, suppression, and repression?
- To what extent are they related to more recent conceptualizations, such as Bion's (1959) minus-K (knowing versus not
knowing), which is often related to the anxiety aroused by sex
differences?

• How are omissions related to Bion's "attacks on linking," in which the links in the relationship between one person and another are destroyed by attacking any meaningfulness in the connection between them, or to Riesenberg-Malcolm's (1989) concept of "slicing," in which meaning is also denuded? These two authors speak of the patients' attacks on the value of meaning, the very meaning *required* for the analyst to do analysis. These attacks then also become assaults on the analyst's sense of reality.

• To what extent is the incomplete reporting isomorphic with the patient's inner experience at the moment?

• Is the omission due to ego weakness or arrest, or is ego functioning temporarily impaired due to some conflict being defended against?

• What is the role of internalization? Miss Atlas, for example, omitted in the style used by her parents, identifying with the aggressors in turning passivity into activity. Mrs. Bernstein omitted in order to keep her grandiose fantasy world as she had reported it to her analyst, and therefore also her precarious narcissistic balance intact.

One needs to understand adequately the patient's relation both to his or her inner world and the outside world in order to treat the patient effectively. Therefore, two other questions the analyst should think about in treating patients who consistently omit are (1) What is the extent of his awareness of others, of the world, of what is happening around him? and (2) What does he scotomatize defensively and then omit?

Similarly, the analyst must ask about the superego structure— whether it is split, fragmented, or intact, harsh or weak—of the omitter. To what extent does the patient experience guilt or shame over the omission, and to what extent does the omission keep fueling the sense of guilt or shame? Neither Miss Atlas nor Mrs. Bernstein was conscious of guilt or shame about their omissions, but they were conscious by way of displacement of these affects into other areas of their lives. The aggression toward the analyst and the analytic encounter that is expressed in omissions protects the patient from experiencing directly feelings of shame or expectation of punishment from fantasies due to oral, anal, and phallic phase conflicts. Their stories are told in such a way that they cannot be perceived as greedy, dirty, or competitive. The displaced senses of guilt and shame, of worthlessness, of not being understood are perpetuated until the omission is discovered and analyzed.

Kernberg (1992) raises important issues about the treatability of those with dishonest transferences who greatly mislead the analyst. He contrasts these patients with others who "may insist, over an extended period of time, that there are issues they will not discuss with the therapist. . . . This honesty in communicating to the therapist their unwillingness to participate in the treatment may permit an analysis over an extended period of time of the reasons for their fearfulness and distrust" (p. 14).

The cases of Miss Atlas and Mrs. Bernstein present us with certain similarities in family history. Both sets of parents were busy socializing and traveling and did not know what was going on in their daughters' lives. They never asked questions. Miss Atlas and Mrs. Bernstein were not held accountable for their actions or their incomplete stories, and their parents did not want to be held accountable either. One might speculate about the parents' pathology in these two cases. Furman and Furman's (1984) concept of "intermittent decathexis," a type of parental dysfunction, seems to be of possible relevance here. The parents' inability to stay focused on their children could have resulted in impaired ego functioning. The Furmans write, "In some child patients the effect of decathexis manifested itself primarily in a difficulty in forming an integrated body image and in maintaining a consistent, sufficient libidinal investment in it to protect themselves from harm and to seek appropriate need fulfillment" (p. 426).

The consequences of parental decathexis or gaps in the parenting function (see also Bach 1994) were impairments in reality-based ego adaptedness, in relationships, in integration, in secondary autonomy of ego functioning, and in the capacity to use analytic insight. We present the concept of intermittent decathexis as one kind of interaction and genetic source that could lead to omissions and other forms of deception. It is among one of the many possible causes that we review in this book.

Miss Atlas, Mrs. Bernstein, and many other omitters describe, characteristically, a phenomenon in their parents that sounds at the very least like a peculiar kind of tunnel vision and at the very most like extreme indifference. The parents did not ask their children what was going on in their lives. In the transference, these patients did not tell their analysts what they needed to know in order to help them. Alternatively, their parents also were intrusive, invasive, and overstimulating at times. Both patients reported accompanying symbiotic or narcissistic fantasies that related to their omissions, namely, that the analyst was all-knowing and did not need to be told what was on their minds. These fantasies were possibly related to the patients' projection onto the analyst of their own wishes for omnipotence and omniscience, and possibly also to their poorly developed empathy for sensing what the analyst might know or not know about them. They also entertained fantasies that the analyst was uncaring and/or bored and did not wish to know any pedestrian details of their lives. Finally, they fantasized that the analyst was intrusive, potentially destructive, and quite primitive and therefore must be kept out.

TECHNICAL CONSIDERATIONS

Patients who regularly omit significant material must, on that account, be understood as having ego impairment expressly in the area of object relations, which requires certain modifications in classical analytic technique. For example, Miss Atlas's analyst found it useful to telephone her after several sessions were missed. Mrs. Bernstein's analyst told her about the theater review she had read and about which she had mentioned nothing. These interventions were intended to lessen the psychological distance between patient and analyst, which might have remained untouched had the modifications not been introduced.

Omissions are to be regarded not so much as direct defenses against the impulses but as more indirect and related to the ego's defenses against the analysis of the impulses; therefore, they are serious obstacles to the analysis. It is recommended that the analyst take an active role and continually ask him- or herself: "Is there more to this than I am being told?" "What hasn't this patient told me?" "Can I picture this patient in his or her life outside my office?" "What hasn't this patient enacted with me (knowing what I know about him or her) and that may be enacted with others outside the treatment?" A common example requiring a translation of these questions into confrontations is that of the patient who splits the transference by telling dreams, fantasies, and memories to friends and relatives, even to the analyst's friends, rather than to the analyst. Confrontations, such as "I have the feeling that something has been left out," and such questions as "What is occurring to you, what are you feeling when you do this?," and "What did you anticipate experiencing with me if you told this to me?," are ways to begin to address and ultimately to interpret these resistances involving omissions.

Some patients keep their sessions emotionally separated from their lives outside of sessions. Some omitters refuse the analyst's recommendation that they come four or five times a week (as did Miss Atlas) and prefer twice-weekly sessions. Doing so enables them to avoid certain material. They cancel, do not show up, or are late and are incapable of giving an adequate explanation. Some play mind games, withholding in order to trick and frustrate the analyst. The analyst who questions them can then be experienced as calling them on the carpet, as a mistrustful parent, a "detective Mom," or an inquisitioner. The analyst must be neutral but firm and pose questions as part of the work that analyst and patient must do together in order to better understand the patient and these typical patterns, which are often analyzable enactments.

Kernberg (1992) recommends taking an active stance with suppressors. Others, such as Giovacchini (1985), take a less active stance, believing that doing so would favor the patient's autonomy. Searles (1986) recommends avoiding giving the patient the narcissistically humiliating message that he is not free associating correctly. Greenson (1967) recommends that patients' secrets be respected and not forced out of them.

In contrast, we recommend that patients be asked to tell everything. That is, patients are expected to follow the fundamental rule and to free associate, even though we understand that many cannot begin to achieve this goal until far into or even toward the end of the analysis. It would seem from the analysis of omitters that they have been functioning too much on their own and do not know whom or how to trust or to feel free if another person knows about them. These are issues to address and to analyze, not to avoid. Of course, issues of timing and dosage must be respected.

As a final point, countertransference problems can arise with omitters, although they tend not to be as severe as those arising with lying patients, for the aggression toward the analyst is not as great (Lieberman 1988, 1991b). Feelings of chaos, of having formed a distorted picture of the patient, of being duped and betrayed, of feeling gullible—all can produce negatively toned feelings, often strong ones, such as rage toward the patient, that must be dealt with by the analyst through self-analysis and not acted out with the patient. Countertransference reactions can be expressed by a series of rationalizations for certain technical interventions, as in becoming overly active, playing "analytic detective," or sharing in the patient's defensive operations and pretending that one did not notice that something has been left out. In his paper, "Turning a Blind Eye," Steiner (1985) describes his reaction to an omitting patient: "In the transference, I was often drawn into various manoeuvres to prevent the cover-up from being exposed and was often in danger of finding reasons of my own for turning a blind eye to uncomfortable facts" (p. 170).

Milder reactions of discomfort have been reported by Lipton (1991), who writes:

> I have analyzed one patient who was the subject of a paper written by another analyst, and often in the treatment I felt under pressure because of knowledge from that paper that the patient had not told me, and did not know that I knew. This factor was a burden on my free-floating attention. I was anxious about the possibility of revealing information from the paper. "Outside," not shared, information, like any secret, creates a barrier to relationships. [pp. 983–984]

The most problematic countertransference with omitting patients is that of the analyst who feels threatened by the possibility that he might be duped and turns a blind eye to that possibility. The treatment in such a case can only lead to pseudo-understanding. It is recommended, therefore, that all of us attempt to address this issue in our daily work.

3

PATIENTS WHO LIE

When my love swears that she is made of truth,
I do believe her, though I know she lies,
That she may think me some untutor'd youth,
Unlearned in the world's false subtleties.
Thus vainly thinking that she thinks me young,
Although she knows my days are past the best,
Simply I credit her false-speaking tongue:
On both sides thus is simple truth supprest.
But wherefore says she not she is unjust?
And wherefore say not I that I am old?
O, love's best habit is in seeming trust,
And age in love loves not to have years told:
    Therefore I lie with her and she with me,
    And in our faults by lies we flatter'd be.

—Sonnet 138, William Shakespeare

Note: This chapter is based on two papers presented by Janice Lieberman, Ph.D.: "The Gullibility of the Analyst and Patient," at the Division 39, American Psychological Association Meeting, San Francisco, February, 1988, and "Technical, Dynamic and Structural Issues with Patients Who Lie," 37th International Psychoanalytical Association Congress, Buenos Aires, August, 1991.

The psychodynamics of patients who lie to their analysts in psychoanalytic treatment have not as yet been examined thoroughly, despite what seems to be the substantial incidence of such behaviors on the part of some of our patients. Analysts usually trust that they are being told the conscious truth and willingly suspend disbelief as they struggle to make sense of their patients' narratives. If they did not do so, their work would be almost impossible to conduct. Although lies are expected of psychopaths, as Weinshel (1979) has written, "there is a comparable 'expectation' that the so-called neurotic, healthier patient will not lie deliberately to the analyst, and the idea that the patient will be assiduously 'truthful' with the analyst is a more or less commonly accepted element of the analytic relationship" (p. 504). Freud (1937) instructs analysts that "we must not forget that the relationship between analyst and patient is based on a love of truth, that is, on the acknowledgement of reality, and that it precludes any kind of sham or deception" (p. 266).

Yet, Freud himself reported a number of lies and lying dreams that were told to him by his own patients (1913, 1920). In *Two Lies Told by Children* (1913), he writes of a case in which a woman's boastful lies masked her feelings about a disappointing father, presenting him to the world falsely as supremely effective. Admitting her deceptions would have been tantamount to admitting her hidden incestuous love. In fact, themes of lying and gullibility are to be found throughout the history of psychoanalysis. The first psychoanalysts in Vienna initially believed that their patients were lying about being seduced as children. And Masson (1984) essentially calls Freud a liar for suppressing the truth about the real seductions of his patients so as to further the acceptance of his theories about the importance of internal fantasy. Eissler's trusting attitude toward Masson, who betrayed him, illustrates the extraclinical gullibility of at least one noted analyst (Malcolm 1983).

We define conscious lying as Fenichel (1939) did: "an untruth in which the subject himself did intend to deceive others with his assertions and did not believe the assertion himself" (pp. 130–131). The kind of lie to be discussed here is entirely *conscious* and *intended*.

In their excellent review of the psychological and psychiatric literature on lying, Ford and colleagues (1988) summarize a myriad of reasons for telling lies: to maintain autonomy, to hurt others, to avoid hurting others, to avoid humiliation or punishment, to gain love, to gain power, to create a better story, and so on. Although the consensus is that, in general, lying is pathological, it can be adaptive in certain instances and may have originated as an adaptation to a pathological situation. Tausk (1933), for one, notes an adaptive function of the lie:

> Until the child has been successful in its first lie, the parents are supposed to know everything, even its most secret thoughts. The striving for the right to have secrets from which the parents are excluded is one of the most important factors in the formation of the ego, especially in the establishing and carrying out of one's own will. [p. 456]

The psychoanalytic literature to date contains references to psychopathic lying and to lying that supposedly emanates from patients' unresolved conflicts organized at the oedipal phase of development. Lies are treated as defensive phenomena. Fenichel (1939) likewise understands the economics of "pseudologia fantastica" to be a warding off of the knowledge of instinctual events. The liar thinks, "As I now take in others, so it may be that I was only taken in when I saw what I was afraid was true" (p. 137). He reports the case of a woman patient, a compulsive masturbator who was fearful of burglars and murderers. Her lies consisted mostly of sexual and self-glorifying boasts. For example, as a child, she lied to her teacher that her class was planning to attack her and that she had seen a ghost. The psychogenesis of her lies was found to be based in having heard horror stories from the family cook. She focused on these stories instead of her own primal scene fantasies. Her father had long talks with her that resulted in her sexualization of talking. Her mother shielded her and helped her ignore reality. In this paper, Fenichel attributes the nonspecific gratuitous lies of the obsessional patient to a substitution of *small changes* and omissions for unconsciously wished for much *greater changes*.

One classical position has been that lying about general matters at large symbolizes specific lies about the genitals. When Mack Brunswick's (1943) male patient accused her of lying, it was as if he were saying, "It is not I who need to deny the facts, but you. And you must deny them for me, for I cannot bear the fact that you have no penis" (p. 461).

Weinshel (1979) interprets the lies of neurotic patients as enabling them to re-enact aspects of the oedipal conflict. Pregenital factors are present but not considered by him to be essential. The lies permit partial recovery of old memories and unconscious fantasies, in some cases screening oedipal and primal scene fantasies. One patient's lie was that she had "nothing" to say, which covered over certain sexual secrets. One such secret was related to her fantasy that the analyst had a crush on her. She felt her parents had lied to her when her mother told her that she and her father were speaking about "nothing," which she equated with their sexual secrets. Another patient circulated little lies about the analyst: that he never said anything, that he said too much, that he told funny stories, that he wore outlandish clothes. Some were partly true, others not. She involved Weinshel in a lengthy analysis of a symptom, of the meaning of a genital itch, and then revealed to him that she had lied about the date of its onset and had distorted other data so as to mislead him. Weinshel understood the genesis of her lie as related to fetishism and negation wherein the lie negates the truth. His theory of lies thus stresses the centrality of fantasies about genital sexuality.

In Blum's (1983) famous case, a male patient about to begin an analysis phoned him and said he could not get to the initial session because "my mother died and I will be in touch with you after the funeral." The patient recontacted Blum a year and a half later to begin treatment and admitted that he had told Blum a lie. His mother was still alive, although his father had died when he was 10. Blum wondered whether this patient was analyzable, but decided to commence the analysis because a preponderance of factors spoke in favor of analyzability. Blum's classic oedipal-phase-centered analysis reveals multiple meanings of the lie. For one, it reveals the lie to be an unconscious confession of matricidal wishes as well as an ambivalent identification with a depressed, withdrawn mother. It enables the patient to deny the oedipally charged memory of his father's death. Blum also understands the lie as a sadomasochistic provocation, aimed at deriding him and making him out to be a fool. Related also are feelings about the patient's mother's colitis. As a child, he often found excrement on the floor when she could not get to the bathroom on time. Her incontinence was met by silence and shame in the family. She also gave herself and the patient enemas. Blum writes that one of the meanings of the lie is "a repetition of the enema trauma, a submission to the therapeutic process followed by defying and deceiving me with the pseudo-production of 'bullshit.' As a faecal object, the lie was 'living shit' and dead loss" (p. 24) , a fleeing from homosexual submission. The patient had an inconsistent superego, failed to master traumatic states, and was burdened by separation-individuation issues.

This patient's history and development were typical of deceptive patients. That is, in deception sadomasochism is prominent, anal fixations are important, superego development is sporadic, and identifications with deceptive parents occur frequently. More recently, work done by object relations theorists call into question the higher developmental level previously attributed to patients who deceive the analyst. O'Shaughnessy (1990) argues that these patients are organized at more primitive levels:

> Because it presents itself in speech, lying must seem to be a relatively mature pathology. Analytic investigation reveals, however, that the fundamental problem the habitual liar is bringing to analysis by lying is primitive, and primarily involves not the truth and falsity of propositions but the truth and falsity of his objects, their genuineness or deceitfulness. [p. 187]

The important roles of separation–individuation, preoedipal conflict, fixations at the oral and anal phases of development, and failure of ego integration in the genesis of lying must be emphasized. Those who lie to their analysts do not seem to have a particularly high level of ego and superego structural development, even though the content itself may be at times oedipal. That is, many turn out to be more primitive in structure and function than they may seem initially. The illustrative examples of this early ego pathology, which follow, are drawn from two cases in which patients in psychoanalytic psychotherapy lied to the analyst. Conscious lying to the analyst can be diagnostic of severe pathology. Better integrated patients, more suitable for classical analysis, usually suppress and repress, rather than omit and lie about what is too painful to admit.

O'Shaughnessy reports several cases in which she became involved in chaotic transferences in which the patient experienced her as her lying mother who could not mother properly. One patient asked to change the time of his session because he supposedly needed to meet the plane of a cousin who was flying to his city. In a subsequent session, this excuse then changed to needing to meet the sister of an old friend who was coming for an abortion and then to the sister of an old friend who had only one leg! The analyst's feeling of being provoked by these lies was additionally exacerbated by her discovery that her patient had given her a false address and phone number. He told her that he did not want to be "rung up and told there was no session." O'Shaughnessy documents the sadomasochistic gratification of such patients, who experienced her interpretations as beatings.

Lies have also been understood as having as their underpinnings fantasies of sexual revenge, as they facilitate the discharge of sadomasochistic impulses. The liar experiences considerable excitement in the telling of lies, in getting away with it, in being found out, in telling more lies, and in the subsequent threat of punishment.

The lie is aimed directly at the one being lied to. It is of course aimed consciously and unconsciously at other figures as well.

The patient who lies makes certain assumptions about the analyst's vulnerability and gullibility. He or she may assume, for example, that analysts are more concerned with the genesis of distorted perceptions and less with the kinds of cues others use to assess a person's character. But it is mainly the nature of the work and the work ethos that predisposes analysts to a vulnerable gullibility. Various conditions of the analytic situation that foster vulnerability to deception, such as the requirement for adopting multiple perspectives, are discussed in Chapter 4 on imposture.

Analysts' gullibility can be supported by the belief that they possess special knowledge of what goes on in others' minds. Farber (1975) has written that "one of the curiosities of gnostic certainty is that it renders the believer so gullible. There are psychoanalysts who will believe absolutely anything a patient tells them about himself provided it is sufficient testimony to his morbid or pathological condition" (p. 23).

The gullibility of the analyst is a special form of gullibility that is not necessarily pathological, but is related more to the life experiences, personality structure, and professional requirements of those who become analysts. The analyst's gullibility is based on the nature of the analytic task, which is to suspend disbelief. It can also be based upon a lack of personal experience with liars and with lying, for the better integrated analyst may lack an internal frame of reference to permit a quick and easy grasp of the sadomasochism or the lack of trust of the patient who lies. Nor can most analysts really understand from inside themselves why such patients lie to them, especially when their lies are gratuitous. The analyst usually does not have an inner frame of reference enabling him or her to really empathize with such patients in their efforts to sabotage the treatment. Instead, he or she must understand the genesis and meaning of their lies from a strictly intellectual framework.

The following case material illustrates some of these points about both the lying patient and the gullible analyst. The lies told to the analyst in our examples seem to be innocuous when compared with the egregious lies cited by Weinshel, Blum, and O'Shaughnessy, and they might even be construed as part of the psychopathology of everyday practice. They proved, however, in each patient, to be reflective of problems, of splits in the ego and superego, and of other serious pathology that had not been addressed in the early phases of treatment, before they were sufficiently understood.

Miss Alexander, a marginally anorexic–bulimic woman, was in a twice-weekly psychoanalytic psychotherapy with a relatively inexperienced analyst. The patient was charming, attractive, and bright, but she suffered greatly from low self-esteem. After several months of treatment, she acknowledged to the analyst that she lied to others regularly, compulsively, and quite gratuitously. The analyst asked her if she had ever lied to her, and from time to time, in the context of the patient's speaking about her lying, the same query was repeated. She vehemently protested, "No, that would be counterproductive." The analyst, she said, was sane, and she lied only to others who were crazy. Those others would get angry were she to tell the truth and the analyst would not. The analyst wished to believe that her patient really did experience her differently from others. Two years passed, during which time Miss Alexander made considerable progress in the areas of consolidating her identity, raising her self-esteem, and improving her relationships with others.

One day she arrived quite late during a severe rainstorm. The vignette that opened this book was based on this incident. The analyst had glanced out from her office window and happened by chance to see her alight from a taxicab with the regal, gracious air that recalled the pathological grandiosity she had manifested from time to time in some of her sessions. She entered the office in a most apologetic manner. She explained that she was late because she had been standing on her corner for a long time, could not find a taxicab, and had walked twenty blocks to the analyst's office.

The analyst was puzzled about the best mode of addressing this falsehood. The lie in this case seemed meaningful and could represent, from what her analyst already knew of her, a masochistic fantasy in the transference in which she needed to present herself to her analyst as pathetic and impoverished while secretly she could bolster an inner grandiosity by putting something over on her. This self-presentation also represented her way of maintaining separateness from the analyst, by contradicting her assertion that she always told her analyst the truth and was having a *different* kind of relationship with her. Miss Alexander lied compulsively to others, but somehow managed to convince her analyst, who had a not too uncommon countertransference fantasy about "rescuing" some of her patients, that she told her the truth.

Momentarily disarmed, and defending against the signal anger and the disappointment aroused in her by Miss Alexander's lie, the analyst did not address this lie during the session. She waited, instead, for the next opportunity, in which she raised the issue of Miss Alexander's ability to pay a small fee increase. Her fee initially had been set at a very low rate because Miss Alexander protested that she could not pay more. Yet, her lifestyle, as revealed in treatment, seemed discrepant with her reportedly low income. When the discrepancy was pointed out, Miss Alexander precipitously broke off treatment and would not deal with her analyst's rather tactful questioning of her veracity. It seemed that the only way she could continue to stay in treatment was if she could fool her analyst as she did the rest of the world. Her precarious psychic balance depended upon her having gullible objects, whom she used in repeated attempts to restore her injured narcissism. In her case, these issues were far more pressing than any dealing with conflict, so that attempts to analyze any possibility that she was disappointed about her analyst's gullibility or was guilty about having put one over on her were to no avail.

As a child, Miss Alexander was a poor eater and her mother force-fed her. She would refuse to eat and instead would sit before a cold and unappetizing plate of food for hours. When her mother succeeded in forcing her to eat, she would vomit, and then her mother would force her to eat the vomit. As an adult she would starve for days and then binge in secret. If her room-mate came home while she was on a junk-food binge, she would stuff the food into her handbag, kept at her side especially for that purpose. In her fantasy, eating in front of another would lead to engulfment, a revival of feelings connected with her mother's smothering response to feeding.

Since in the transference she experienced her analyst as the force-feeding bad mother who made her eat her own vomit, her lies possibly represented her wish that her analyst, in a reversal, would become the one who ate the bad food. O'Shaughnessy's patient lied in a similar fashion: the lying symbolically repre-sented a wish to feed her bad food. Her interpretation of a dream containing this wish was: "The two pigs you feed stand for me, whom you feed with your talk. In this dream you are bringing your fear that I won't know the difference between your real communications and the other stuff, the rubbish" (1990, p. 187).

Miss Alexander was conscious of a fear that others would be angry with her if she were to tell the truth and envious of her if she admitted to having anything good. But once again, her nar-cissistic vulnerability outweighed her guilt and conflicts about duping her analyst, and interpretations close to O'Shaughnessy's paradigm could not reach the basic character pathology in which her lying was embedded. Unconsciously, the lies kept her at a safe distance from others, who represented her engulfing and force-feeding mother. The lies also enabled her to repeat a chronic experience of guilt over having been such a bad daugh-ter. Harsh superego lacunae were the analogue of her weak ego structure. Like other patients who deceive, Miss Alexander's narcissism was quite impaired. She told the analyst that she would feel like a "nothing" if she did not lie. Lies helped her maintain control over others. She said, "It's the way I have power over them. I control the impression I make on them. If I were to show myself as I am, I would lose control."

As a result of the work accomplished during the time she was in treatment, Miss Alexander was able to meet and to become engaged to a young man whom she experienced as kind and quite suited to be a potential mate. However, she felt that she had to conceal from him the fact that she was in treatment. Final interpretive efforts centered around the various meanings of her lying about her ability to pay and about her need to lie to her fiancé, who evidently was to replace the analyst as her gullible object.

A second patient, Mrs. Boxer, grew up in a family in which she was grossly neglected and at times physically abused. As an infant she was sent to live with an aunt, for her mother was unable to manage her care along with the care of her older children. She came for twice-weekly psychoanalytic therapy in order to deal with the breakup of her marriage. She was unable to work even though she had had sufficient education to find employment on a professional level. She did, however, seem to be able to provide good enough care for her young son. Through an unconscious identification with her son, she was attempting to provide for herself a second and more benign childhood.

Mrs. Boxer reported panic attacks and migraine headaches—at home alone or when driving—in which she became convinced that she was going to die. She would then cease all activity and enter a state of withdrawal. Analysis of this defense revealed that rather than take active steps on her own behalf she would, as she put it, "kill herself off," deaden any spirit or initiative, and enter into a private world of fantasy. She began doing this as a child, when she was virtually imprisoned in a room all day adjacent to her bedridden, poorly groomed, chronically depressed mother. As she began to tell the analyst about her split-off fantasy world, she increasingly became able to take some concrete action in her life. Fears then emerged that, were she to find a job, she would not have time to live in her inner world—a dream world that was the only place she believed she was allowed to actually "live." The patient's sweet demeanor and her rich associations elicited in her analyst a strong sense of trust in her as well as respect for her courage.

Then the analyst stumbled upon a lie. The patient telephoned the day after a job interview and asked in a pleading voice to be given a later appointment that day, for she was in the nurse's office at her son's school with a migraine headache and could not possibly arrive on time for her early morning appointment. At this point, the analyst viewed the request as an ordinary one, and in fact had at that moment no other time to offer her. A few minutes later, however, another patient canceled his hour, and the analyst uncharacteristically, in what she soon understood to be a counterenactment, telephoned Mrs. Boxer at the nurse's office at her son's school in order to offer her the later hour. The nurse said that she had not seen Mrs. Boxer at all that day.

The analyst found herself to be quite unclear as to why Mrs. Boxer had lied or what to do about it. The patient's lie seemed to derive from her ongoing fantasy that she was sick and in need of care. She seemed to be splitting the transference by going to the school nurse instead of to her session for some kind of help. The lie could be further understood from the material of her most recent sessions, which had to do with her anticipated move forward into a good job. By lying, she could shut her analyst out of her world. If she did not need to do this, she could have simply cancelled her session. The analyst hypothesized that she did not want her to know where she was as a way of regaining control of her world. In the next session, the analyst told Mrs. Boxer that she had phoned the nurse and reported to her what the nurse had said. Mrs. Boxer said it was the wrong nurse, that when the analyst called, she was in the school cafeteria with a different nurse. The analyst decided not to pursue the matter further, although she believed that Mrs. Boxer was just elaborating on the original lie. She planned to analyze the lie when the patient was in a more integrated state. She did, however, alert the patient that she was aware of the inconsistencies in her story. She also interpreted her need to gain control by avoiding contact with others in the *displaced transference*. Eventually, Mrs. Boxer was able to make use of this understanding of her lies, confirming the interpretations made by the analyst as she began to speak of compensating for shame experiences with stories she told to her relatives about exciting friends and experiences she had had when in fact she had had neither.

DEVELOPMENTAL CONSIDERATIONS

Most of the writings in the psychoanalytic literature assign the genesis of lying to the vicissitudes of the oedipal phase of development. The lie is understood as serving to maintain repression and as being organized around oedipal phase fantasies (see Blum 1983, Freud 1913, Fenichel 1939, Greenacre 1958a, Mack Brunswick 1943, Weinshel 1979). For psychological studies of the development of lying and deceit, see de Paulo (1982), Peterson and colleagues (1983), and Piaget (1965).

In the cases of Miss Alexander and Mrs. Boxer, however, issues of separation-individuation predominate. These two lying patients feared attachment and tried to avoid feelings of closeness and tenderness with the analyst by maintaining separateness through their lies. The underlying fantasies reflect oral and anal phase conflicts and express a wish to gain control over frustrating, controlling, internalized objects that are at times overly intrusive and at times totally absent.

Patients who lie repudiate any gratification to be obtained from the object, anticipate pain, and seek to separate from the object by means of lying in order to protect and/or maintain self-cohesion. The one who is deceived is then put into the position of holding onto the liar by believing the lie. If the deceived one confronts the lie, the liar will probably leave the relationship. This is an important factor characterizing the basic dyad of liar and gullible one, of deceiver and deceived.

The liar takes an active stance in his symbolic feeding of bad food to another, as in the example of Miss Alexander. The liar struggles to detach, to separate, to avoid symbiosis. Supporting this thesis is Greenacre's (1945) explanation of the psychopath's particularly pressing need for separation from the mother, due to the particular kind of narcissistic attachment the typical mother of the psychopath forms with her infant, which arouses aggression and impedes the internalization process.

Early in the psychic development of lying patients such as Miss Alexander, Mrs. Boxer, and others, some overwhelming trauma, either shock trauma or strain trauma, occurs. The developing ego is weakened in some way that leads to certain truths becoming too threatening, too intrusive, and too stressful to be assimilated, contained, and absorbed. Miss Alexander was traumatized by being force-fed and ridiculed. Mrs. Boxer was beaten, restrained, and abandoned. They both deployed dissociative defense mechanisms in order to protect their parents from their aggression, which was then displaced through lying to the one deceived. So, as much as lying patients may fear the closeness of symbiosis, they also need to protect the original parental objects. When this particular early preoedipal conflict is handled by means of dissociative defenses, a tie to the analyst as a new object who can be trusted is most difficult to establish, and the success of the treatment is often put in jeopardy. We note that patients who lie often seem to be extremely trustworthy, for the part of them that lies and presents itself to others is dissociated from the part that is aware of the truth.

Rosenfeld (1987) reports a case of a psychiatrist patient, Caroline, who was put in jail for selling drug prescriptions, a side of herself concealed from her analyst:

> The lying in these cases is so complete and so consistent that the analyst is generally taken in and does not know that he is being lied to. With Caroline, one never had the feeling that she was lying. She seemed to have split off her criminal and murderous self utterly, so that when this was acted out disastrously in real life it was uncontrollable. [p. 136]

Patients who lie very often suffer from identifications with parents with faulty egos and superegos who have lied to them or disappointed them; they then tend to defensively idealize the parents (Gottdiener 1982). Bollas (1989), in his analysis of Jonathan, a lying psychopathic patient, finds the lies to function as reparative and control measures:

> It is only in phantasy that Jonathan can evolve a completed experience with an object, as the continuous interruptions by the parents of their potential use as Jonathan's object left him bewildered and compelled to create an alternative world. He lies psychopathically (automatically) because lying functions as another order of self and object experience, an order that consistently helped him to recuperate from the actual absences of the parent. [p. 179]

Thus, lying is encompassed by living itself. The lie exposes to the other the betrayal by the parents.

Parental complicity in the development of the proclivity to lying is also addressed by Deutsch (1923) who writes of the narcissistic gratification accruing to parents who used their children as extensions of themselves:

> Those [parents] who were lied to by their children took refuge from sad reality in the fantasy structure of their children. The crudest outside assistance was sufficient to cause their morbid imagination to believe in the reality of what they were told. They believed because they wanted to believe, because they saw their dreams realized in the lies they were told. And only an intuitive awareness of this fact enabled the liars to be believed in. [p. 150].

Although one would naturally assume that lying patients have weak superegos, in cases such as those of Deutsch, the superego *structures* are harsh while the *contents* lack prohibitions against lying. These are in fact cases of harsh superego development with concomitant superego lacunae relating mainly to content that give a misleading overall picture of superego laxity. Patients whose parents encouraged lying unconsciously seek punishment when their lies are discovered and by this means

fuel their chronic sense of guilt about having told the lies. Superego lacunae are evident in cases where parental gratifications
from the child's lying interfere with the development of superego contents that forbid them to tell lies, as in Deutsch's example.
Considerable ego impairment is involved, for these lying patients
cannot foresee the negative consequences in store for them, including frequent recurrences of negative therapeutic reactions,
eventuating in the invalidation or destruction of their analytic
treatment.

TECHNICAL ISSUES

Special technical difficulties arise in the psychoanalytic treatment
of lying patients, especially in connection with our axiom that
lies should be dealt with as soon as they are recognized, within
the limits of dosage, timing, and tact. Strong countertransference
reactions are provoked both by the lie and the need to acknowledge it and must be analyzed as soon as possible so that a neutral stance can be maintained. Patients who lie are particularly
prone to reactions of narcissistic rage, shame, and humiliation
and, by their use of projective identification, sudden suspicion
of the analyst when they become aware that the analyst is aware
of the lie.

Because lying patients typically use dissociative mechanisms,
their commitment to treatment is often tentative, and they sometimes precipitously terminate when realistic perception becomes
unavoidable and the split-off aggression inherent in the lying
becomes accessible.

Analysts work in the context of a contemporary culture in
which confronting lies is not generally supported. In Victorian
times, it was a challenge to address sexual wishes and fantasies,
which were not at the time discussed publicly. Today, the analytic challenge may center more on controversial issues of morals and ethics because we tend not to confront these matters in
social settings. Many of us have actually been punished for con-

fronting a liar, especially a parent who lied. In analytic treatment, however, a lie must be called a lie. The impact will be attenuated when the psychodynamic context is permitted to emerge and be interpreted.

We aim in psychoanalytic treatment to help our patients achieve better integration and to avoid further shock to the ego. The issue of timing and dosage is relevant here. We are often reluctant to analyze a lie or a denial of a lie because of the impression that the patient's ego is not strong enough at that moment to tolerate the threat of a fantasized loss of the analyst. We are also reluctant because of our concerns about bringing on depression, as in the case of Mrs. Boxer, the patient who lied about why she needed to have a later hour. Helping the patient gradually become aware, as opposed to forcing upon him a sudden awareness, is the path to take. For example, the analyst can point to inconsistencies in the story as a way of coming closer to confrontation. In this way, the rage toward the analyst that emerges in the form of a displacement from the self or from the object will not be so overwhelming as to disrupt the working alliance. A steady softening of the denial of the lie should enable the patient to avoid experiencing the shock trauma that is often a repetition of past trauma.

Kovar (1975) describes the technical dilemma of the analyst:

> Does he in the service of speaking the truth tear his patient apart, or does he in the service of compassion relinquish his patient to the falsity of the lie? . . . In his efforts not to hurt he is aided by a nomenclature which includes a variety of euphemisms for lying and deception. Whether he uses these only to help organize his own thinking, or out loud to help organize his patient's, he is unlikely to think of his patient as lying and even less likely to speak to him about his lies. [p. 42]

Soon after the analyst becomes aware of a lie, he or she should bring this awareness into the session in a neutral manner. He or she must not withhold, but instead deal actively with the matter. The analyst's withholding of her awareness of Miss Alexander's lie led to the building up of too much aggression, both in the transference and in the countertransference, and may very well have contributed to the patient's premature termination.

Strange derailments in the treatment, unusual or unexplained absences or cancellations, and inconsistencies in the patient's reports might alert the analyst to the possibility that a patient might be prone to telling lies. When a patient seems comfortable with such inconsistencies, it should be understood as a signal that the synthetic function of the ego is impaired.

In making recommendations for the treatment of lies, Kernberg (1975) observes that patients who habitually lie project their own attitudes regarding moral values onto the therapist, whom they then see as dishonest and corrupt. Such patients wish to assert superiority over the therapist, deflect his or her efforts, exert control, and protect themselves from the dangerous retaliation they fear from the therapist should he or she know about matters they wished to hide. They consciously exploit the psychotherapeutic relationship for ends other than receiving help. When such attitudes persist, treatment cannot take place. The analyst must vigorously interpret the lies in the transference. If these attitudes can be changed and a climate of mutual trust instituted, then treatment can proceed.

An assessment of treatability must be made for the patient who has told too many flagrant lies to his analyst (Blum 1983, O'Shaughnessy 1990). Reality testing may be too deficient for such patients to profit from psychoanalytic treatment. Lies destroy meaningful interpersonal links, and there is a point at which there is too much meaninglessness to continue. These are issues that bear upon the personality and persistence of the analyst as well as that of the patient.

Weinshel (1979) describes a common reaction of righteous indignation in his patients, along with their allegations that he had violated some pact by confronting their lies. Weinshel does not allow himself to be deflected by this accusation and presses on to analyze the patient's experience that the analytic contract has been violated. In a typical case, he finds that the patient's reaction is a repetition in the transference of a covert pact in childhood when neither the patient nor the parent was ever to speak about having engaged in some kind of forbidden relationship.

In cases in which fees are reduced in order to accommodate patients who enter treatment reporting an inability to pay or who request a fee reduction during the course of treatment, risks of creating a therapeutic impasse are taken, since some percentage of these patients may be lying. The lie, guilt about the lie, and attempts to be consistent with the lie, such as concealing pay raises, purchases made, and trips taken, all serve to defeat authentic treatment. Slakter (1987) discovered his low-fee, unemployed patient exiting from a department store laden with packages and then entering a chauffeur-driven Rolls Royce that had his initials on the license plate. Slakter's confrontation in the next session resulted in his patient's tearful relief at being found out. His imposture was due, he explained, to his fear that the analyst and others would only be interested in him for his money. The admission of the lie was couched in yet another lie. We naturally would want to explore these kinds of explanation that could be either extensions of the original lie or new lies to deal with the painful sequelae of older ones.

Countertransference

Countertransference reactions to lying patients can be quite powerful and usually emerge quite abruptly. The ego boundaries of these patients are usually weak and fluid, and they utilize the defense mechanism of projective identification, projecting onto the analyst disowned aspects of the self. Once aware of the lie, the analyst's neutral, benign, passive stance may abruptly shift to one of shock, outrage, or rage if he enacts what the patient is provoking in him.

Bollas (1987) reports feelings of frustration, anger, personal futility, and sadness after being lied to. It is essential that a thorough analysis of the meaning of the lie to the analyst be immediately undertaken so that he can regain his neutrality prior to dealing with the lie with the patient. Gediman (1985a) had a similar reaction to her impostor patient: "Why did I let things develop to the point where . . . I began to see him as the incarnation of that very evil he had been proclaiming as his ego ideal?" (p. 922).

After the lie is exposed, the analyst must be able to tolerate the sudden perception of himself by the patient as bad, guilty, sadistic, cold, and/or distant. Patients who lie react with righteous indignation when faced with the reality of their lies. They experience the analyst as distant and punitive as they relive and, by way of the transference, project their childhood experiences of lying and/or being lied to onto him or her.

O'Shaughnessy (1990) describes the lie as having damaged her equilibrium, making her incapable of working, depriving her of needed knowledge, and getting her to take the lies as truth, "so that I actually became a partner in a perversion of the analytic relationship" (p. 184). She experienced herself as a "corrupted container."

The analyst's task is to detach enough from his experience of hurt and assault to feel neutral and benign enough to treat the patient. If the analyst remains too angry, treatment may have to be discontinued, for as Blum (1983) notes, the working alliance "develops with difficulty . . . where there is a lack of mutual trust and where prevarication provokes countertransference" (p. 18).

Those analysts who have heretofore taken pride in their insight into human nature feel caught short by the sudden turn that knowledge of a lie told to them brings. Analysts' work involves knowing, and what they believed that they knew is suddenly invalidated, affecting their own narcissistic balance. Lies are often told to analysts in cases in which they have had to work very hard to supply meanings and synthesis to material that is meaningless and fragmented.

Weinshel (1979) describes our ambivalence about moral virtues:

Honesty and the capacity to tell the truth are highly venerated moral virtues in our society, but like so many of the moral virtues, our relation to them is both inconsistent and paradoxical. While we respect those who demonstrate these virtues, it is not infrequently a respect commingled with some cynicism and mistrust. The feeling that the truly honest man is somewhat gullible is not a rare attitude limited to the antisocial fringes; and a modern day Diogenes is likely to be viewed as a quixotic figure open to condescension or gentle ridicule. [p. 523]

We believe that Weinshel does not sufficiently take enough into account the *directness* of the aggression toward the analyst in the "real relationship" when he considers that the lies patients tell to their analysts are not moral lapses but useful analytic data as focal points for the reconstruction of early trauma. They are, of course, that, but they are also more than that. This view of lies as purely and solely transferential phenomena denies an aspect of the *direct combat* with the analyst about the worth and validity of truthful discourse and of analysis as a vehicle for uncovering and facing the truth. It also denies that aspect of the analyst's response to the patient as an ordinary person, as described by Winnicott (1947).

The lie may be experienced as a greater assault than other hostile manifestations. The analyst is hurt because the very heart of his or her work is to search for a meaningful narrative for the patient. The lie renders the work meaningless. Because the lie cuts to the quick of what the analyst values most, some analysts defend themselves, perhaps against envy of the patient's freedom from moral prohibition, perhaps against partial identifications with the primitive gratifications to be gained from lying, by being taken in by the lie. It would not be unusual for analysts unconsciously to envy the patient's freedom to lie, for their work ethic and general moral integrity do not permit them to lie in their work. And so, in the worst case, the perverse dyad of liar and gullible analyst is perpetuated.

Trust

Essential to the understanding of transferential and counter-transferential aspects of lying in treatment is the elucidation of the role of trust in the working alliance and of establishing trust as one of the goals of psychoanalytic treatment. Without a certain degree of trust in one another and in the worth of what is being said by both patient and therapist, analytic work becomes meaningless (see Isaacs et al. 1963). And if at the end of treatment a patient cannot yet trust those around him, the work has also been of questionable value.

Analysts take an essentially trusting stance in their work. They assume that their patients tell them the truth, and they struggle to make sense of what they tell them. They often work after the analytic hour, without pay, by thinking, reading, and consulting with others. This work reflects their trust in what is being told to them.

Patients in analytic treatment are called upon to be perhaps even more trusting than the analyst, for they are asked to open up their deepest wounds, their skeletons in the closet, their deepest shame-ridden experiences for the analyst's scrutiny. They are asked to do this and to trust that what they say will remain confidential. They do this in the hope of getting well. These parameters of analysis often seem to be of dubious value to some patients, especially at the beginning of treatment. Yet, they are asked to continue to pay, to invest emotionally in an analyst who remains anonymous. Patients can only proceed according to their perceptions, which are colored by need, by the affects aroused in the regression, and especially by the transference. Some patients learn for the first time in their lives to trust others as a result of being in treatment, only to find themselves betrayed in the world outside. Paradoxically, they must learn to withhold trust in order to be able to trust safely, at least transitionally, until they have accurately assessed the nature of those with whom they are dealing. Just as they learn early on not to leave cars unlocked on city streets, they need to learn to suspend trust in new relationships, with lovers, employers, and friends, until they know more about them.

Analysts, too, must learn to suspend some degree of automatic trust in their patients, for as Marcos (1972) has noted:

> To be able to believe the patient's productions seems an indispensable premise for the building of a sound doctor–patient relationship; on the other hand, unconditional credulity could encourage lying and stimulate deceivers. On that ground, a certain amount of "constructive skepticism" appears as a necessary ingredient in this unique relationship. [p. 200]

PATIENTS WHO ARE GULLIBLE

Isaacs and colleagues (1963) define gullibility as "a readiness to believe that what is wished for, often unconsciously, is to come true, despite reasonable unlikelihood. It is thereby a readiness, a desire to be deceived" (pp. 360–361). From time to time, we have been in the somewhat uncomfortable position of serving as observers of our patients' gullibility. There are occasions, for example, in which we have begun to believe that a patient's spouse is having an affair, whereas the patient, by all indications, believes that his or her spouse is working late at the office. There have been instances in which a patient is asked to lend money to a friend, and it seems apparent that the money will never be returned. As analysts, we must maintain neutrality while analyzing what in the patient interferes with the exercise of good judgment and reality testing. Our task is to help our patients act in less self-destructive ways, to get in touch with reality—however painful—without our making any *direct* statements about the patients' lovers or friends. At such times, we scrutinize what we have heard in order to be absolutely certain about our perceptions. We ask ourselves whether our patients know more than they are admitting to us and whether they could be transferentially inducing us to behave as untrusting or infantilizing parents.

Gullible patients unconsciously wish to believe the lies they are told and do not welcome the truth. Their analysts, idealized at the beginning of treatment, eventually come to be experienced as aggressors, as the bearers of bad tidings, or as envious enemies who rain on their parades.

Some patients are gulled constantly and know it, and others refuse to acknowledge being gulled even when they have suffered the negative consequences of their naiveté. Analysts can at times foresee negative outcomes while their patients continue to blind themselves through denial and/or rationalization. We propose here certain analytically correct techniques to deal with such situations.

Miss Smith, an obese laboratory technician with poor body hygiene, greatly feared the sexual advances of men were she to look and smell attractive. Despite the psychotic-like quality of her physical appearance, she was quite related, affable, and astute in her observations of those around her and made correct judgments about other patients she encountered in the analyst's waiting room. She described the foibles of those around her with hilarious humor and keen psychological sophistication. Despite her astuteness, however, she was an easy mark for down-and-out friends who borrowed money from her and did not return it, for artists who sold her their unmarketable art, and for bosses who convinced her to work long hours for low pay.

Guilt, masochism, and fear of object loss were very much involved in her surrender to these people. Her conscious fantasy was a symbiotic one, of being one with her mother. In her analysis, she traced her gullibility to an infantile feeding experience in which she was put into a high chair for hours at a time, wrapped in a blanket, and fed constantly. She was unable to express her rage about her frustrated needs for autonomy and locomotion and instead had idealized her mother.

In the transference, the analyst too was idealized. Miss Smith's latent aggression and mistrust manifested themselves constantly through maneuvers that put the analysis in jeopardy, for her income barely covered the cost of treatment. At any moment, whenever progress was made, a periodontist could be relied upon to recommend a $10,000 gum treatment for Miss Smith, or a veterinarian could be counted on to recommend an expensive cardiac surgical procedure for her aging dog. Miss Smith was extremely gullible, and after a while her analyst began to experience herself as gullible in believing Miss Smith's catastrophic stories. She also experienced herself as helpless about being able to anticipate the onset of these events or to interpret their meaning to the patient. Treatment was constantly on a precipice of derailment. The analyst felt she had to suppress interpreting her patient's wish to save her precious dog's life as a defense against the treatment, since the patient's love for her dog reigned supreme in her life. The analyst's position as one who must be paid for analytic work became problematic for Miss Smith, for the patient's parents were untrusting people who viewed outsiders with suspicion. They constantly scrutinized the analyst and undermined the patient's trust in her because they were convinced that she was seeing Miss Smith solely for the money she would receive. Their suspicions reflected the flip side of Miss Smith's gullibility. The patient's descriptions of her interactions with various friends, bosses, and other doctors led her analyst to be suspicious that *they* were heartlessly divesting her of funds, a countertransference reaction undoubtedly induced by the patient.

After many years of treatment, a number of productive sessions led the patient to the sudden realization that her mother was *not* devoted to her best interests, as her mother had always led her to believe. She also suddenly understood that her father had always been, and still was, extremely sadistic and that her best friend was not at all to be trusted or believed. These realizations, experienced as trauma, eventuated in her leaving treatment precipitously by making a Sunday afternoon call to her analyst's answering machine. She demanded in a tone that had to be respected that the analyst not try to contact her. She evidently needed her gullibility more than the truth the analyst was calling for in the treatment.

Mr. Levine, an attractive and extremely successful entrepreneur, was considering divorcing his wife of fourteen years in order to join a woman with whom he had been having a three-year affair. He was guilt ridden about his affair with this woman, whom he experienced as extremely gratifying, especially when compared with his rigid, aloof, and withholding wife. He sought analytic treatment in order to feel more able to initiate the divorce. He was extremely uncomfortable and guilty about the lies he told his wife as to his whereabouts when he was with his lover. Affairs often serve the unconscious purpose of generating and maintaining guilt feelings. Those who lie to their spouses very often deny all possibility of having been lied to and betrayed themselves, and see themselves as the sole guilty party in the marriage.

After hearing an interpretation that addressed the above dynamics, Mr. Levine informed his wife of his wish to divorce her. She said she did not wish to divorce him and wanted to keep the marriage intact. At the same time, however, she began to spend many weekends and sometimes weeks away from their apartment, leaving no telephone number where she could be reached. She told him that she was away on business, but also that she earned no income during this period of time. She continued to live in a most luxurious manner and ran up extensive bills that he paid. The patient refused to pay attention to the increasingly obvious signs that his wife might be seeing another man, was staying at that man's home, and was hiding income from him. He continued to feel guilty about his own behavior. In this case, his gullibility served the function of denial, of perpetuating a sense of guilt, and of self-punishment that could be acted out in his giving over to his wife more money that he consciously thought she deserved and that she would be legally entitled to in the eventual divorce agreement.

The analyst had to monitor her interventions in order to maintain analytic neutrality while confronting her patient's defensive denial and self-punitive tendencies implied in his continuing to believe his wife despite contrary evidence. The patient felt guilty that he no longer loved his wife and about his anger toward her. When he was in his teens, his mother had had an affair, attempted to divorce his father, and found that she could not. His identifications with both mother and father were apparent, as was his need to maintain the fantasy of a good mother/wife in order to avoid dealing with his unconscious disappointment in his own mother for her betrayal of his father.

Mr. Levine terminated treatment precipitously with no prior warning the day after he signed the divorce agreement, whose terms were surprisingly fair to him. The discovery, in treatment, of his wife's lies to him aroused tremendous rage toward the analyst as the bearer of bad tidings, and was experienced as destroying his denial as well as his omnipotent fantasy. He thus experienced the analyst as an aggressor, as attacking his wife whom he needed to hold onto as a good object. He blamed the analyst as if she had been the cause of his wife's deceptive behavior, for in the treatment he had to give up whatever illusions he had about her.

The word "gulling" has the oral connotations of swallowing and guzzling. When a gullible person realizes that he or she has been told a lie, the aggression he or she has managed to ward off is then experienced internally, possibly re-creating an earlier trauma of abrupt disillusionment, as if he or she had been suddenly poisoned. The impulse is to spit out and to reject the truth. Believing a lie can result from a fixation, usually the outcome of overindulgence at the oral phase of development, as in the case of Miss Smith, the orally indulged patient whose ability to pay for the analysis was constantly threatened by her indulgence of her friends and her pet. As in any case of parental overindulgence, one might rightly suspect a reaction formation against unconscious aggressive impulses as motivating the parent. Paradoxically, then, overindulgence may be experienced unconsciously as a punitive act of aggression, and indulgent acts toward friends, family, and pets are double edged in their functions of gratification and punishment. As Isaacs and colleagues (1963) note, "The gullible person perceives the world through unrealistic hopes, for safety and comfort, for pleasure and gratification" (p. 366). The gullible one struggles, by believing the lies, to avoid separation. He "eats" the implausible lie as a way of sharing the lie-fantasy with the liar. Gullibility can also be described as anal-retentive in nature. Something bad and alien (the other person's lie) is held in. When the lie is discovered, previously suppressed anal-expulsive aggression helps to evacuate it, as in the case of Mr. Levine. The gullible person usually feels ashamed that he has taken in the lie that was inflicted on him so shamelessly. The liar can be seen as symbolically depositing his fecal product in the gullible one's ear. The gullible one, on the other hand, feels powerless, manipulated, and fecalized.

Often the liar's sense of genital inadequacy leads him to symbolically cut down, render inadequate, castrate, penetrate, or rape the gullible one so that he can feel that he is the adequate one. The gullible one attempts to attach by believing the lie, taking its contents seriously, giving it meaning and significance. Paradoxically, the lie very often has no meaning and reflects only the liar's despair. Ford and colleagues (1988) comment that "the psychological impact on the receiving end of lies can be devastating. Major life decisions may be based on false information believed to be correct. Lies may also have adverse effects on liars themselves" (p. 560). Kernberg (1975) observes that compulsive liars have little awareness of how those they lie to experience the lie. Words cannot bring them what they need, and therefore, it does not really matter what they say.

Often in lying, the symbolic meaning of the words in the lies themselves is not what the lie is about. What it is about is the enactment of an unconscious fantasy via the way the words are used in the lie. We end with the philosopher's *Paradox of The Liar*: "A man says he is lying. Is what he says true or false? If true, it is false; if false, it is true" (O'Shaughnessy 1990, p. 187).

4

IMPOSTURE, INAUTHENTICITY AND FEELING FRAUDULENT

The world is crowded with "as if" personalities, and even more so with impostors and pretenders. Ever since I became interested in the impostor, he pursues me everywhere. I find him among my friends and acquaintances, as well as in myself.

—Helene Deutsch

This epigraph introduces Helene Deutsch's famous paper on the impostor. Her words imply the universality of impostorous tendencies. In this work, she writes of the *sadomasochistic excitement* of impostorous states, which leads to heightened sensations and heightened narcissism and is characterized by a strong libidinal investment of the self. Deutsch, alone in her time, was able to have a long period of observation and treatment with a patient who was a true impostor. Her patient was a very anxious man, who became even more so during the supportive treatment.

Note: This chapter is an expansion of a paper by Helen K. Gediman with the same title, published in the *Journal of the American Psychoanalytic Association*, 1985, volume 33, pages 911–935.

Much could be learned from his history about the early development that is common to many impostors and imposturous individuals. Like many other impostors, he was libidinally and narcissistically indulged by his mother, so that he grew up with the expectation that he did not have to make many efforts on his own behalf. Like many other impostors, he succeeded, to a point, in getting others to collude with his wishes. This ability to control others helped consolidate anal sadistic character trends, which led him often to regard others as objects to be manipulated toward his own ends and to disregard them as human beings in their own right.

In this chapter we deal with imposturous tendencies as *ubiquitous* and *heterogeneous*, and we aim to take a new look at the concept of imposture by studying its various manifestations in the psychoanalytic situation. We subsume the category of the true impostor under the most general category of imposture. A true impostor is an individual who assumes an identity or title, a literal name of someone other than him- or herself. The true impostor misrepresents himself and typically has a severe character disorder (Moore and Fine 1990). He or she, but most often he, passes himself off incognito, which is often the only way he can function. The impostor engages in delinquent, psychopathic, or sociopathic acts or other criminal behavior with the conscious and deliberate intention to deceive in ways facilitated by his false identity. Greenacre's (1958a) impostor patient, for example, impersonated a doctor and served on hospital staffs with only the medical training he had received as an orderly during World War I. His skill and persuasiveness were combined with stupidity and a profound need for self-betrayal.

Imposturous tendencies occur in a variety of personality disturbances and situations, from the least to the most pathological. At the least pathological end of the spectrum is the promotion of illusion and disguise within the bounds of creative art and play. At the other end is the true impostor. The as-if personality, which has been subsumed under imposturous conditions, falls somewhere in between these two ends. This pathology is an identity disturbance characterized by unstable and unintegrated identifications. While the true impostor pretends under literal cover of someone else's name, the as-if personality, lacking a cohesive identification, unconsciously takes on the color and style of admired individuals through mimicry and imitation (Deutsch 1955, Greenacre 1958a, Ross 1967). They may role play facilely, but generally do not come to the attention of the law for any reason. The as-if personality resembles Winnicott's (1960) *false self* which feels more real, subjectively, than the nonexperienced potentially integrated true self. An important aim of imposture is affirmation of the false self by a real or imagined audience that can be fooled, duped, or deceived. Such affirmation by an audience serves defensive, integrative, narcissistic, and self-cohesive functions, and gratifies the instinctual drives.

Imposturous tendencies may enter into neurotic character and compromise, but are most likely to reflect more severe character pathology. This pathology usually involves an ego function disturbance with multiple shifting identities and subsequent problems in the subjective sense of the reality of the self and objects. Imposture in a person undergoing analysis is, however, not just a function of individual character and psychopathology; it is also a function of certain inevitable requirements of the analytic situation, to be reviewed shortly, which constitute a "pull" for its emergence. Vulnerable individuals or those with neurotic or, more likely, character pathology involving imposturous tendencies will respond to this pull in revealing ways.

We review here three cases in the context of a spectrum of imposture, broadening our understanding of that problem and increasing our recognition of important clinical variations.

The idea of a spectrum, and it is difficult to say whether we should regard different varieties of our phenomenon as falling on a continuum or as discontinuous, should be particularly compelling for analysts who have experienced difficulties in coming to definite diagnostic conclusions in assessing certain manifestations of inauthenticity in their analysands. Consider a patient who appears shifty, in the sense of easily shifting roles, or of going from one accented speech pattern to another, or any variety of quick changes in self-presentation. Is this patient a true impostor, assuming multiple false identities in order to deceive deliberately? Or, is this patient an as-if personality presenting with unstable, shifting, unintegrated identifications along with a preponderance of imitative tendencies? Or, is this a patient who tends subjectively to *feel* fraudulent and imposturous when to the objective observer he or she is not? Is the deceit we think we see not deceit at all, but something related rather to the more or less normal promotion of illusion, as in art and play? Apparent lies and deceit may also function defensively to disguise unconscious wishes and fantasies, that is, "something untrue may be represented as something true, to make it possible to represent something true as untrue" (Fenichel 1939, p. 130). Such apparent lies may be looked upon as genuine lies by some in that they seek to conceal by presenting something other than that which would be most useful to the analytic work. The cases we present illustrate particular and important variations of imposturous tendencies.

The continuum implied by these questions, ranging roughly from the most to the least pathological forms of imposture, covers the pathology of the psychopathic impostor who may assume a false identity for conscious and deliberate purposes of deception, through the pathology of a variety of heterogeneous individuals who manifest a shaky identity sense. It includes those who are particularly vulnerable when empathy and multiple, shifting identifications are required by certain situations, such as being an analysand or learning to do analysis. Finally, it refers to those who have problems with illusion and disguise within the range of the psychopathology of everyday life. Most of the psychoanalytic literature to date approaches the problem of imposture from the viewpoint of pathology. This work approaches the problem from the other direction of the more average-expectable end of the continuum as well.

These attributes of an altered subjective sense of reality of the self, along with disturbed self and object representations, have also been discussed extensively in the literature on narcissistic and borderline personalities. Although some of the individuals we are discussing may be diagnosed as belonging to these categories, our emphasis is decidedly not on placing imposturous tendencies within any one specific diagnostic category. Our perspective here, which also has a history in the literature, is on ego function disturbance as arrayed on a continuum along which any individual may be assigned a place, according to the degree of disturbance (see Bellak et al. 1973, for a comprehensive review of this tradition).

DIAGNOSTIC ISSUES

The first problem we face is differentiating the psychopathic from the nonpsychopathic. There is an illusory quality to "created experience" that stands in the borderland between reality and authenticity, on the one hand, and between unreality, inauthenticity, and outright lying, on the other. That illusory quality creates difficulties in certain differential diagnoses. In identifying psychopathy, we are prone to make false-positive as well as false-negative assessments. That is, it is easy to be conned by real psychopathy into overlooking something psychopathic that is present, just as it is easy to assume falsely the presence of psychopathy when it is not present.

Abraham (1925) presents the very first psychoanalytically informed study of an impostor, seen first by him in 1918. This impostor had impersonated prison officials and obtained money under false pretenses. He was convicted and imprisoned, but released in an amnesty at the end of World War I. When Abraham saw him again in 1923, he had improved markedly and was leading a responsible life. He had married an older woman, a "little mother" whom he called "Mummy," repeating in this way an oedipal attachment to his own mother who had both indulged and rejected him as a child. This was a vulnerable solution, as he had become dependent on a woman who was likely to die before him and defeat his self-serving purpose of marrying an older woman in the first place. In fact, he had continually abused the trust of others, with the unconscious motive of taking revenge on the parents he felt had rejected him. Abraham concludes that the man's temporary and repeated successes at deceiving were associated with strong unconscious guilt feelings that had to bring, as an act of self-punishment, a rapid end to his happiness.

Abraham's case highlights the problem of distinguishing elements of neurotic pathology, such as the hysterical symptom formation of that form of lying called *pseudologia fantastica* (Fenichel 1939, 1945) that we reviewed briefly in Chapter 1, from the serious character pathology of deception found in the true impostor. Yet another differential diagnostic issue lies in teasing out the more serious ego pathology from the structural transference–neurotic elements in both the true impostor and others with imposturous tendencies. In our focus on the neurotic aspects, we are concerned with the possibly innocuous, or at least more universally found needs for punishment involved in lying, forgery, swindling, and so forth. These criminal acts are sometimes motivated by a neurotic need for punishment, as among "criminals from a sense of guilt" or "those wrecked by success" and in other neurotic character problems (Freud 1916). Some masochistic characters and obsessional neurotics under the domination of the repetition compulsion are also to be found among impostors and the imposturous. The imposturous are driven to produce *illusion*, rather than *substance*. They suffer from a neurotic fear of commitment to well-developed and sustained interests when such responsible commitments are unconsciously equated with monstrous crimes for which they would not want to risk being caught. Better to be caught at the lesser crime of imposture, as uncomfortable as that may be. Such neurotic conflicts were found among Freud's criminals from a sense of guilt.

Related to these imposturous patients are those who consciously feel and fear they are fraudulent when they are not.

Neurotic and Deficit Aspects
of Imposturous Tendencies

There are those who might argue in either-or terms about what is more central to imposturousness: is it a deficit, a fundamental ego pathology, such as a fragmented identity sense due to developmental arrest, or, if not that, then is it the neurotic need for punishment for excessive forbidden gratifications of whatever nature? Generally speaking, deception in its more severe manifestations suggests character pathology. Nonetheless, it is wise not to avoid too strict a polarization, for even the most character-disordered patients also suffer from neurotic conflict, such as a neurotic need for punishment for oedipal wishes. That is Freud's position in his work on character types, and it is also adopted by Greenacre (1958a). Her researches reveal that impostors tend to have mothers who are openly critical to their sons about their fathers, calling them ineffectual, who actually often desert their families. The mothers are often overly attached to their sons, contributing to their development as "oedipal winners." Thus, she discovered a constellation of what seem to be oedipal issues, yet she also notes that "the acting out of the impostor is largely an attempt to achieve a sense of reality and competence as a man more than to claim the mother in any deep sense" (p. 112).

This recognition of narcissistic and of ego and structural issues along with oedipal content underscores the complexity of the underlying diagnostic difficulties. A tendency toward polarizing neurotic and character pathology biases our outlook; it is best to examine the problem from multiple, complementary viewpoints, thereby taking into account the mutual influences of both ego pathology and neurotic conflict. For example, in considering developmental arrest or deficit—that is, the well-known characterological disturbances of imposturous individuals—and conflict as complementary points of view (see Gediman 1989), it is important to recognize how ego function disturbances such as failures in internalization, identity diffusion, and ego fragmentation may also serve multiple functions in neurotic compromise formations.

Five important related attributes of an altered subjective sense of reality of the self seem to be aspects of imposture in many of its variations. These attributes range from what is behaviorally observable to what may be inferred about complex dynamics and psychopathology. The first is verbal fluency, facility, and fluidity; the second is a hypertrophied development of a limited kind of empathy; the third is a quality of dilettantism, involvement in esoterica, and artifice; the fourth is an intense disturbance in the sense of identity manifested in multiple identifications and fragmented, largely imitative, noninternalized role-playing; and the fifth is a paradoxically heightened sense of reality accompanying what Eidelberg (1938) has called imposturous "ego states."

As for the first, the astounding verbal mimicry and fluency, Greenacre (1958b) notes that impostors conspicuously use words with punning variations and substitutions, often with names through which nuances of change of identity may be implied. Among the imposturous, that fluency may deteriorate, under pressure, into fluidity, glibness, or disjointed and confused speech. Anais Nin (1959), in her novel about artifice, *A Spy in the House of Love*, portrays such gibberish so well in her heroine Sabina's verbal stigmata: "she behaved like someone who had all the symptoms of guilt . . . her unpremeditated talk, without continuity; her erratic and sudden gestures, unrelated to her talk; the chaos of her phrases" (p. 3). She continues, "And when in desperation he [the lie detector] clung to the recurrences of certain words, they formed no design by their repetition, but rather an absolute contradiction" (p. 5). The "lie detector," a character in the novel, could not, after hours of detection, tell whether she was an actress, or wanted to be one, or was pretending.

The second common feature characterizing the disturbed reality sense of the imposturous appears as an excessive empathy, or, more accurately, empathy-like responses, limited to areas of highly selective, often beautifully attuned, circumscribed, but fundamentally "unprocessed" telepathic-like forecasting of what the person believes the other expects of him or her. This excessive, even uncanny attention to the expectations of others has been noted by Khron (1974), who describes how certain patients regularly put into words the private associations of the therapist just as the therapist is having them. They show a heightened vigilance both to the superficial peripheral aspects *and* the primitive unconscious of others. Furthermore, he notes that this so-called borderline empathy is not unique to borderlines, but occurs among many others who have difficulty perceiving the more enduring, characteristic, consolidated ego attitudes of others. Many people with imposturous tendencies do seem to catch on with extraordinary quickness to what they believe the other is thinking and feeling, both at the most superficial and at the most unconscious levels. Their own shaky and fragmented identity sense would account for difficulties in perceiving the ego-integrated aspects of others. As keen and as sharp as their responses may be in picking up details and certain nuances in the lives and activities of others, particularly those they simulate, they may be, at the same time, utterly obtuse in other areas. That is, they ultimately show a *failure* in empathy. Very specific and detailed examples of this peculiar form of hypertrophied empathy are presented in Chapter 5, which deals with the supervisee who "empathized" in this way with her supervisor in an attempt to learn psychoanalytic technique.

The third characteristic, the unmistakable artifice and inauthenticity in the typical failure of empathy that is so characteristic of imposture, is often masked behind esoterica. The imposturous person, as well as the true impostor, then can count on not being discovered because of an ability to pass him- or herself off, consciously or unconsciously, as having expertise that the average listener could not be expected to evaluate for genuineness or authenticity. We are familiar with glib talkers working in certain fields, sometimes including psychoanalysis itself, in which the area of expertise may be esoteric enough or the linguistic conventions so idiosyncratic as to permit "creative" deviations from the ordinary. Such esoteric fields provide a haven in which inauthenticity may nestle unnoticed for long periods of time.

The fourth characteristic, an intense and circumscribed disturbance in the sense of identity, is manifested in multiple, fragmented, and shifting identifications on an imitative level. It was Deutsch (1964) who pointed out that the as-if personality can exist only by identifications. Ross (1967) suggests that such shiftiness in identifications is not merely an ego function deficit, involving pathology of the self, but it also serves adaptive and defensive functions. For example, agreeing with everyone ingratiatingly may serve as imagined protection from attack; the rapid sequence of identifications may be a means of appeasing people.

Paradoxically, many individuals with these five disturbances in the sense of reality experience themselves as most *authentic*, subjectively, when they are acting imposturously; they often feel as though they are presenting to others with artifice and phoniness when they are in fact functioning at higher, more integrated levels that reflect more consolidated identifications! Some people, for example, are unable to acknowledge real giftedness as their own, imagining instead that they are inauthentic plagiarizing swindlers of other people's ideas; they themselves are unable to distinguish their authentic from their inauthentic being. The true impostor described by Deutsch (1955) never feared exposure when he was a swindler, but felt like an impostor and inauthentic when he did honest work. Various explanations have been offered for this paradox. Greenacre (1958a,b) theorizes that a narcissistically heightened sense of reality may derive, for some, from the sadomasochistic excitement of imposturous states. Others (Deutsch 1942, Ross 1967) have suggested that guilt related to oedipal conflicts accompanies the imposturous individual's attempts at higher-level functioning. Therefore, such a person feels subjectively more real with a false self presentation than as a true self, for defensive reasons.

It goes without saying that, with the typical failures in ego functioning, the failures of constancy in object cathexes, and the subsequent failures of internalization seen in identifications that never progress beyond the early stages of imitativeness, there would also be serious lacunae in superego formation (Jacobson 1964). Like ego attitudes, the morals of the imposturous are poorly internalized or consolidated. They tend to be simply imitative reflections of good and bad, the content of which varies with the momentary object of identification. Along with disturbances in ego functioning and identity, then, is a malformation of the superego, conscience, and ideals (see Greenacre 1958a).

All of the aforementioned disturbances in the sense of reality of the self and the world usually have been attributed, in developmental terms, to a fixation at the 2- to 3-year-old developmental level of imitativeness and primary identification, with a persistence of the simple mimicry of that very early type of identification. No one, however, with the possible exception of Greenacre (1958a), has suggested what maladaptations during that phase are specific to the development of imposturousness. She suggests anal identifications where the devalued stool substitutes for the phallus, contributing to devalued images of self and others, and "the sense of the sublime power of an illusory counterpart" (p. 110). One finds as a rule, in the phase-appropriate ways in all object-relations development in all kinds of diagnostic patterns, the same processes one finds among the imposturous: multiple identifications, the self and object poorly differentiated, and object constancy not yet established—at one time or another. Such processes also characterize a range of later outcomes. Thus, those conditions may be necessary, but hardly sufficient to account for the specific outcome in question.

THE ANALYSAND AS IMPOSTOR

As a critical requirement of the analytic situation, the analyst and the analysand *must* focus on multiple shifts from inner to outer reality, *must* aim toward constructing multiple and changing life histories, and *must* adopt multiple points of view and perspectives for understanding current life problems and conflicts. Such required shifts in perspective often involve shifts in identifications that are essential for empathy and insight and for the process to move on. The fluidity of perspective *required* in learning to be an analysand, an analyst, and a supervisor might in itself constitute a pull for a certain, it is hoped transitory and reversible, as-if behavior, phenomenologically speaking. This modus operandi perhaps could even encourage the average participant to *feel* like an impostor from time to time. In those with significant imposturous tendencies, the pull could constitute a more serious danger.

In dream analysis, for example, we encourage our analysands to see multiple and complex aspects of themselves as represented in their various roles and other self-representations that are portrayed by various characters in the manifest dream content. There may be disturbances in the sense of reality as the analysand contemplates his or her self-created dreams and fantasy interpretations. It would not be too far-fetched, then, to think of the patient as feeling somewhat imposturous as he or she has certain reactions to these self-creations, which may or may not precipitate a troubling sense of identity, according to how potentially fragile that ego function may be.

We are reminded of the writing strategy of D. M. Thomas (1981), author of the novel, *The White Hotel*, which features shifting versions of reality that represent shifting versions of narrative truth, depending on the viewpoint of the particular protagonist. Certain patients with unstable identity formation were made extremely anxious by that novel. Our perplexity about that very facility of portraying shifting versions of truth, the so-called Rashomon phenomenon, inspires us to seek ways of differentiating out constructionism, pluralism, and other multiperspectival views of reality from the psychopathology inherent in pathological, imposturous renderings of reality.

In the following case summaries, each analysand shows significant disturbance in one or more aspects of the sense of reality discussed above.

Mr. Green

Mr. Green was brilliant and facile with the surface meaning of words and ideas, and gave the impression that he had a capacity for depth of understanding as well. He was the child of socially marginal, nomadic parents who themselves were prone to living a life of unreality, falseness, and deception, which he had internalized as part of his character. Although in fact ashamed of their quirky lifestyle, he also turned his humiliation into an idealization along the lines of a family romance fantasy; with this reversal, he embarked on a course of imposturous and narcissistic personality development that easily moved on to the psychopathic when his grandiose attempts to fool others had failed. He learned very quickly during his childhood development what was expected of him in mainstream culture, and as an analysand did the same. He manifested what LaFarge (1994) has labeled a typical imposturous transference, presenting as a "caricature of what he imagined a good analysand was supposed to be, producing a detailed facsimile of analysis in which the analyst's interpretations served to give his performance an exciting stamp of reality" (p. 12). He brought in dreams with the kind of symbolism that nearly always seemed to confirm his female analyst's tentatively offered speculative hunch about his unconscious conflicts. He himself became an expert at responding in an empathiclike manner to his own primitive unconscious, but did not have much insight into the ego and superego aspects of his functioning. For example, in a typical early session that dealt mainly with his fear of there being nothing there if he were to associate freely, he reported a dream he entitled "Premature Pontification" in which female genitals on a screen merged from light into dark into nothingness. "Ah," he said, "I concede with relish to your analytic prowess in connecting 'nothing there' with castration. You have a point and I become more diffuse and blobby." The more playful he became at punning, the more he became obtuse to whatever meaning could be attributable to his failure to make more than small payments on owed fees. This delinquency, he insisted, was irrelevant analytically, and the problem was that his analyst was too uptight about it.

As an analysand, he seemed a natural until one discovered that his associations to and his glib interpretations of his dreams and symptoms were replete with ridicule of psychoanalysis, and of his analyst personally, as in the example above. His fantasies of writing literary treatises for esoteric periodicals on the unconscious meanings of his symptoms and dreams included wishes to expose the analytic process as fraudulent. He initially sought treatment because of a serious writing inhibition, for although he had ambitions to write in his area of expertise, he could not write, but would verbally infuse others with his esoteric ideas. Although an academician in a prestigious institution, he was hired without ever having taken the requisite graduate courses, an almost unheard-of feat in his field and in his school, where all teachers are required to maintain certain standards through continuing education and written work. It became apparent in the course of the work that he had misrepresented himself by offering false credentials to both his analyst and his employers, all of whom felt deceived and angry when they eventually learned that what they originally respected was a sham and a scam. Like LaFarge's Prof. G., he tended to substitute an empty performance for the real thing, but when confronted with his deceptions, he suffered acute anxiety about being exposed as a "psychological" fraud and impostor. His anxiety did not seem to derive from a guilty conscience, but from a reality-based fear of losing his job.

Nevertheless, he insisted such fears were neurotic and should be analyzed away.

Why was he kept in analysis for as long as eight months? He expressed conscious concern, anxiety, and guilt about his super-fluency of language and dialect, which he correctly believed was a sign of his instability as well as a talent. He was concerned about some real-life tangles that his predilection for the illusionary over the workaday and his outright deceptions through artifice had led him into. He worried that he lacked solidity, believed he assumed various roles too well and convincingly. He complained of a compulsive quest for ambiguity about who he actually was because of "a fear of consequentiality." The presence of real psychic pain provided potential motivational inroads, and kept his analyst interested in doing analytic work with him. Addition-ally, he was accustomed to having others *wish* to take him seri-ously, and his analyst was no exception.

Meanwhile, the analysis itself was being ridiculed by his deter-mination to experience it as inconsequential, and the analyst was being ridiculed for taking him or anything in the world as seri-ous, solid, or real or, to use his term, as "consequential." A series of fantastic coincidences had made it impossible for him to pay his bills on time, to write checks that did not bounce, or to get to the bank before it closed. In the beginning he managed enough partial payment for his analyst to believe the matter was an analyzable one, *especially as he would link it to apparently mean-ingful psychological content.* Psychopaths typically pay the first bill to throw the other person off, which is just what Mr. Green tried to do. In fact, he was like LaFarge's imposturous patient who fabricated changes in his schedule and life in order to trick her into changing arrangements that were part of the initial agree-ment. Mr. Green would wax philosophical that all the coinci-dences preventing payment must be further evidence for the uncanny feeling with which he started analysis: it was irrespon-sible for him to be in such a luxurious, truth-focused treatment modality because he did not deserve it as a person. He felt like an impostor to be working at anything so genuine when he him-self suffered from *painful* but *apparently self-serving feelings of unreality*. Like LaFarge's Prof. G., he wished to substitute an empty performance for a genuine effort, avoiding any deep kind of involvement.

After a while, however, this motivational inroad itself proved inaccessible. Not only did he disclaim all responsibility for his financial swindling of his analyst but he also told her that if she would simply *trust* that the money would materialize without a plan, the treatment would proceed much better. It felt so pro-saic to him, so bourgeois, so opposed to a greater sense of moral-ity to plan about money, for after all, as psychoanalysts all know, money is equated with feces and his values were set at a higher level. He prided himself on his sense of true morality, in con-trast to her trivial morality: he valued certain types of murder-ous acts as aesthetic zeniths, though he, personally, probably would not kill or cause physical harm. To be concerned with a payment was not part of his enlightened moral code, whereas to cleverly fool others was. Mr. Green held that if he were going to commit an infraction of consensually held moral and ethical codes, it had better be a *big one*, to be done in excess. This per-verse grandiosity, according to his value system, would lend his criminally tinged act some aesthetic credence so that, philosophi-cally speaking, it would be on a higher plane than a mere petty malfeasance. What others might question on moral grounds and consider as arrogance, grandiosity, even criminality, this patient rationalized as meeting elitist esoteric standards of excellence, reflecting an ego ideal not atypical for impostors.

In some ways, Mr. Green was reminiscent of Freud's patients described in *Criminals from a Sense of Guilt* (1916b). In discuss-ing some character types met in analytic work, Freud refers to misdeeds committed by patients during the time that they were in analytic treatment. Paradoxically, these misdeeds, rather than producing a sense of guilt, arose from guilt and were accompa-nied by a sense of relief for the doer. The basic mechanism, ac-cording to Freud, is the displacement of guilt from the great, but unconscious crimes of parricide and incest onto the lesser crimes, such as Mr. Green's high-mindedly rationalized nonpayment of fees. In this way, said Freud, the guilt that was fixed onto the lesser crimes serves to keep unconscious the greater fantasized crimes of killing the father and having sexual intercourse with the mother. Of course, what Freud was describing was a neurotic criminality, and not the criminality of the severely character disordered, and he himself wished to leave it to further research to decide how many criminals are to be reckoned among these "pale" ones. By now, it seems clear that our research findings among psychopathic characters is extremely meager when it comes to the count of true impostors and other criminals who suffer from simple neurotic pathology. Mr. Green indeed was covering up parricidal wishes in his panoply of morally and ethically deviant behaviors used to advance himself professionally by destroying the values of his academic mentors. However, the oedipal content did not in any significant way reflect the pathology of the neuroses that could be resolved simply by analytic interpretation of motive and defense, by conflict analysis. The oedipal content in his underlying unconscious parricidal wishes was vastly complicated by the overlay of psychopathic and deviant character formation, as is generally the case among those committing more serious misdeeds of deception.

Mr. Green patronized his analyst's insistence that he look into these matters analytically. Why did the analyst let things develop to the point where she not only could identify him with confidence as an imposturous psychopath but also began to see him as the incarnation of that very evil he had been proclaiming as his ego ideal? To paraphrase one of Freud's "Exceptions," Shakespeare's *Richard III* (see Freud 1916), since he could not prove himself lovable, he was determined to prove himself a villain. It is important to wonder whether something beyond the analyst's countertransferential reasons for wishing this patient to be a good analysand was involved in her being that willing an *audience*, hoodwinked into denying his psychopathy because she was moved by his obvious pain, his motivation, his eagerness to be an analysand and to attend sessions, and his attempts at small payment from time to time. That he suffered pain engaged the analyst's compassion and delayed her recognition of the super-ego defect, of the aggression, and of the sadomasochism in the psychopathic transference. He must have known that *uncon-sciously, his analyst, like many others, wanted to believe him.* After all, he suffered, was potentially creative, appeared to understand about analysis. He learned the language quickly. He knew she did not want to believe he was psychopathic, but he also knew she would not continue to work with him if she came to believe that this were truly the case.

So far, we can observe several trends described in Chapter 1 in our introductory remarks about deception in the analytic encounter. The imposturous analysand gulls a potentially gull-ible analyst, gratifying his aggressive wishes in an assault on her sense of reality and on their presumably joint attempt to estab-lish meaning in an analytic dialogue. Instead of being charmed when she discovers that the analysand is presenting a caricature of an analysand, she feels disturbed when his deceptiveness is exposed. Second, an imposturous transference develops into a truly psychopathic one, in which the imposturous individual receives sadomasochistic gratification from his knowledge that he is deceiving the analyst. Sensing that the deception is no longer effective, that his charm has been exposed as deceit, he angrily moves into a psychopathic mode to avoid the pain inherent in the failure of his narcissistic defenses. We analysts do tend to overlook superego pathology when we sense pain. Consequently, we fail to remain adaptively skeptical and, in well-meaning attempts to be helpful, persist in our endeavor well beyond the point at which we could be reasonably hopeful about its outcome.

An interesting aspect of this case was that Mr. Green became more verbally fluid as the problem with the owed fees contin-ued. He would offer garbled and contradictory accounts of his financial situation, tending toward the deteriorated verbal flu-ency of unsuccessful imposture. His view of himself shifted more to the criminal and away from the troubled. From the beginning, he expressed fears that he labeled as neurotic; the entire analysis would be an attempt to unmask and punish him for a crime he felt guilty of. We might characterize his deception as quintessentially that of a masquerade, caricature, and mocking impersonation of a good analysand.

Although Mr. Green conveyed the impression at first that he suffered from a neurotic criminality from a sense of guilt, from a classic success neurosis, and from a quest for talion castration associated with his "fears of consequentiality," he was unable to sustain that impression. Some aspects of a repetition compulsion underlying neurotic repetitive criminality from a sense of guilt did indeed seem to be present and, in the beginning, made the differential diagnosis between psychopathic impostor and masochistic character with self-punishing tendencies difficult to make and at times arbitrary. Much of the associative material he presented turned out to be based on some recent readings of Freud, which he understood superficially, and seemed to be part of an imposture at being simply a neurotic patient as well as a planned mocking of psychoanalysis. But more than that, those tendencies expressed his conflicting fears and the corresponding conflicting wishes of being unmasked as illusory, empty, and only role playing, both in his profession and in being an analysand. He was gifted, as well as a pretender, but when expected to follow through with the responsibilities attendant on acknowledgment or acceptance of the giftedness as his own, he imagined himself to be what he at times did indeed become: a swindler, plagiarist, and, like Woody Allen's Zelig, a "chameleon" man of the world. Operant here were both the dynamic reasons connected with the wish–fear conflict of being wrecked by success, as well as the "prestructural" pathology of self-fragmentation, of too many hacked-up identities.

It would be difficult to settle the differential diagnosis question of what is primary, the structural defect or the need for punishment. We are dealing here with the too fluid linguist, the person of nonconsolidated identities who aimed to set this liability to his own advantage, deceptively, by turning his lack of integration into a performance of pseudo-virtuosity. He engaged in a scam in the analysis as well as in his profession. And he was not entirely without guilt, despite the primitive form and the convoluted content of his idiosyncratic morality, for he feared being wrecked by his deceptively earned success. It is we who tend to dichotomize our patients into either-or categories. Mr. Green's failure to complete his job requirements and his subsequent falsification of his credentials were related to his failure to take analysis seriously. These deceptions seemed to express some primary aggression and were certainly an attack on his analyst's sense of the real and true. These aggressively motivated falsifications also related to his need to see serious responsible work and roles as something superficial—a game, a fad, an illusory indulgence of the idle rich. As his status as mentor and as analysand both stimulated grandiose fantasies, it simultaneously provoked unbearable humiliation and fears of inconsequentiality, just the opposite of his professed fears of consequentiality.

It is not at all unusual for such an intellectually fraudulent person to gravitate to environments that permit the fraud to flourish. These are the "countercultures" that are inhabited by enough people who share the same pathology and engage in the mutual seductions and the narcissistic pact that reinforce the fraudulence. Mr. Green, and others like him, repetitively provoke people in authority, whom they had previously hoodwinked, to feel negatively toward them eventually. They can succeed in provoking the deceived ones into becoming "lie detectors," who subsequently try to catch and dismiss the perpetrator of deceptions. The impostor's victim shifts from being the gullible one to being the angry, even revengeful one, when the imposturous deception has crossed the boundary of libidinal and narcissistic seduction and moved into the area of gross deception and obvious aggression. The fear of possible inconsequentiality evolves eventually into an actualized fate of inconsequentiality.

The moments of seriousness and commitment to the analytic work were troubling to Mr. Green mainly in that they
seemed to interfere with his capacity for maintaining the illusions he required for a reasonably cohesive sense of self. He
had a genuine panic reaction about some indiscreet sexual
behavior in his personal life and wished to hold his analyst
responsible, seeing her as a magical, omnipotent mover, cho-
reographing those self-endangering actions he wished to disclaim in order to keep the whole analytic endeavor on an illusory, unreal plane. He was projecting, thereby, his own wishes
to be omnipotent onto the analyst. His failure to commit himself seriously to the work of analysis and to obtaining credentials for his profession resembled, superficially, a transference
"success neurosis," but at its core, his wrecking of his chances
to advance himself reflected a profound need to negotiate life's
hurdles only marginally. This was one more way that he could
maintain an illusory identity, but one that held him together.
As Greenacre (1958a) notes, a heightened, rather than a dimin-
ished, subjective sense of both reality and identity accompanies
the success of the fraudulence of imposturous claims, especially
when an audience is effectively fooled. Mr. Green seemed compelled to sabotage the analytic work as it moved in the direction of strengthening a subjective sense of authenticity of both
himself and his relationship with the analyst. These problems,
along with the delinquencies around the fee, made it impossible to continue with him in treatment. The hope of fulfillment of his professed career and analytic goals resulted in a
shift from an imposturous to a psychopathic transference and,
as has been mentioned earlier, the analyst's feeling of betrayal
and hopelessness about a positive analytic outcome. Charles
Brenner, in his discussion of an earlier presentation of this
case,[1] characterizes the patient somewhat dismissively as a
"deadbeat," suggesting that the attempt to understand the com-

---

1. This refers to an earlier version of this paper, presented by Helen K. Gediman in
1983 at the Association for Psychoanalytic Medicine.

plexity of Mr. Green's deceit from a psychoanalytic viewpoint might be an exercise in futility.

Traditionally, analysts have had an automatically negative reaction to the diagnostic label, psychopathy, and have tended to prejudge those with serious superego pathology in ways that can preclude analytic understanding. Analysts are particularly pessimistic about outcome, not just because they have been gulled, but because such deceptive patients lose trust in those very individuals they have gulled through their imposturous grandiosity. It is true that very few analysts admit to treating criminals, cads, scoundrels, and deadbeats. Most of the well-known works on imposture, even if written by psychoanalysts, are not based on data from psychoanalytic treatment. These cases, cited by Greenacre (1958a) include Titus Oates (1649–1705), George Psalmavazar (1679–1763), James MacPherson (1736–1796), and Thomas Chatterton (1752–1778). Chatterton is also the subject of a psychoanalytically informed study by Kaplan (1989). Another example is to be found in Geoffrey Wolff's (1979) *The Duke of Deception*. Analysts experience a significant degree of embarrassment in admitting to colleagues that they have been the victims of any kind of deception. In fact, Mr. Green was dropped from treatment because of nonpayment of fees, and did not respond to repeated attempts of the collection agency that the analyst engaged to recover what she was owed, even with the threat of a lawsuit after the court ruled against him. She took the loss. The aggression reached its target. Yet, we are still hopeful that an appreciation of the complexity of the psychopathic impostor's character can be of great general value in the psychoanalytic treatment of deception.

Mrs. Hodges

By way of introduction to the next illustrative case, a particular variant of the role of illusion in the lives of the imposturous must be reviewed. This variant encompasses fantasies that a sense of fragile emptiness and incompleteness can be corrected by some symbolic representation of an "illusory phallus." We have already described this pattern in Chapter 3 in our discussion of Miss Alexander, the patient who felt like a "nothing" when she did not lie. Greenacre (1958a), in particular, has noted that the impostor feels incomplete, anxious, and fearful when not involved in acts of imposture; these feelings are reflected in an "ego hunger" and a need for completion in a particular way: union through identification. Patients with imposturous tendencies often feel incomplete and complain of there being nothing there, even when they are functioning well, objectively speaking. Their characterization of these self-states is not simply an endopsychic perception of emptiness, worthlessness, and defectiveness, which would underpin what Greenacre (1958a) called "ego hunger," but it is also clearly referable to a sense of genital inadequacy, which is usually unconscious. That is, certain individuals with deficiencies in their sense of identity also experience themselves, consciously or unconsciously, as being deficient with respect to genital adequacy. Action experienced as inauthentic is equated, unconsciously, with an illusory but harmless phallus. This symbolic imagery is less threatening to the subjectively experienced self-integrity of certain imposturous individuals than the more genuine acts. The more genuinely self-assertive acts might spark conflicts about exhibitionism (see Conrad 1975) and arouse castration anxieties. This subjective sense of both personality and genital deficit defended against phallic exhibitionistic anxieties and seemed to pervade the feelings of a woman who shall be called Mrs. Hodges.

Like Mr. Green, Mrs. Hodges suffered a writing inhibition[2] that, upon analysis, could be understood as related to a deep-seated fear of writing under her own name. When she did put

---

2. It is probably no mere coincidence that three of the patients discussed in this book, two in this chapter and one in the vignette of Mrs. B. in Chapter 2 on omissions, suffered from writing inhibitions. Although we have not studied in depth the relation of this symptom to deception, the connection promises to be a fertile field for future study.

her name to her work, she feared that she was imposturous. Her symptom could be understood, more so than for the other two analysands, Mr. Green and Mr. Ingersoll, whose case will be presented shortly, in classical oedipal terms. The active claim of authorship on her part was for her unconsciously tantamount to a parricide, for she was deeply guilty about her high literacy level, one that her less educated mother had promoted self-sacrificially. Competent performance was also related to castration anxiety around "phallic exhibitionism," whereas stagy dramatic playing at being smart or smark-alecky did not unconsciously stimulate fantasied dangers of castration or loss of love. She yearned for a male analyst, one who would require nothing of her and from whom she could soak up the "analytic mystique" in safety. With her own female analyst, she felt doomed to hard work and to analytic "stupidity."

Mrs. Hodges was creative, inventive, and a brilliant mentor for her junior colleagues whom she assisted in accomplishing their writing aims. But she could only put pen to paper with her own ideas if "forced," symbolically "raped" into delivery by a strong male figure from whom she craved completion and mirroring acceptance and whom she could imagine as the true author. Mostly, she played dumb, a particular form of deception among certain women who masquerade as stereotypic women to avoid phallic anxieties. She did this with one particular male colleague whom she idealized and with whom she carried on an active correspondence and who was for her an alter ego. His affirmation of each and every sentence was her condition for adequate performance. He also served as an illusory phallus, an imaginary companion, a symbiotic parent, a narcissistically invested mirroring partner whom she actually provoked, like a ventriloquist, into putting her truly original thoughts and words on paper, as though they were his, not hers.

Her manifest craving for this man's validation was, in one respect, an expression of a kind of twin fantasy—that is, the wish for completion through primary union and identification—although in another respect it expressed her need for an illusory phallus. Analysis revealed this twinship or merger condition for performance to be a particular version of feeling imposturous; in psychic reality, she was unable to affirm writing under her own name alone, for when she did, she imagined, for defensive reasons, that she was being fraudulent.

This pattern partook of a form of reverse imposture based on a *fear* of being imposturous, which in turn was based on a fragile sense of identity, a constellation described by Greenacre (1958b) in her discussion of the young Fritz Kreisler. As we mentioned in our introductory chapter, Kreisler wrote his own compositions, but claimed publicly that he had only edited them. He actually attributed the authorship to others who were older than he and were already very famous composers.

This reverse imposture or, more accurately, reverse plagiarism, a form of imposture, served Mrs. Hodges, as Greenacre believed it did the young Kreisler, by warding off the anticipated castration (or abandonment) for oedipal victory. In addition, she connected pleasurable moments in writing with forbidden masturbatory pleasure.

Mrs. Hodges feared to expose herself under her own name. The only way she could display her own creative power was to convince herself that someone other than she should be named to receive title for it. For her own defensive reasons in the unresolved oedipal battle, being publicly acknowledged, even as an adult, as superseding the parental generation, had to be regarded as imposturous. This patient's conflicts suggest certain superego pathology common among those who believe they are deceptive when they function effectively. She was concerned manifestly, in a hypermoralistic way about deceit, as are people who would *never* tell a lie, even a white lie or a tactful omission. Hypermorality, in her case, served as a defense against exhibitionistic impulses and fears of the calamities that would befall her if she were too phallic.

The case does not seem to be one in which superego lacunae were immediately manifest in any significant measure. The patient's oversolicitous and depressive attitude toward her ill and dying mother, however, suggests a reaction formation against hostile wishes and a mobilization of superego guilt. Close contact with her dying mother may have reactivated murderous and incestuous wishes along with the terror of killing and of losing her mother. She must also have felt that she was doing something bad when she "betrayed" her parents' religious beliefs by marrying someone from another faith who had only contempt for her religious background. In her case, feelings of inauthenticity coincided with actual inauthenticity when she, a potentially competent and effective woman, impersonated and masqueraded as an ineffective one. Now that women are being accepted more into traditional male roles, and now that there is some foreseeable possibility of the demolition of the built-in barriers to all levels of success, we are likely to see these conflicts emerging with substantially different content. That is, in contrast to Mrs. Hodges, certain high-powered women in prestigious, high-paying executive positions, experience inauthenticity in the belief that they are merely impersonating high-powered men. Some even masquerade as men, adopting their style and mannerisms in an act of true gender deception, but their feelings of inauthenticity are displaced onto actual and authentic successes.

Mr. Ingersoll

A less obvious form of imposture is to be found in a male patient, Mr. Ingersoll, a braggart, a poseur, and a claimer of expertise when he was in fact only average in his cultural accomplishments and obviously dilettantish. It is noteworthy that, like the artist, Arshile Gorky, to be discussed in Chapter 6, he changed his name, a form of repudiating the hated and dangerous aspects of his early identification with his father. Some "two-timing" of his wife kept him on the razor's edge and chronically excited. The excitement kept him alive not only sexually but also in the deepest narcissistic core of his being. Mr. Ingersoll seemed to be repeating periods of his childhood and adolescence in which any form of forbidden sexuality was met with unusually severe beatings from his father and perverse encouragement from his mother.

His subjective sense of identity and his sadomasochistically exciting two-timing were so interconnected that he hid from his analyst his plan for a long-awaited vacation, in one of those omissions that were discussed extensively in Chapter 2. Planning a vacation actually represented for him a step toward maturity and possible resolution of a deep-seated oedipal conflict he had been working on in treatment. For years, he did not take stock of his financial assets, for even having assets felt imposturous to him—a decided oedipal triumph, as was the vacation. But to hide his money, as though he had stolen it, like the chronically postponed vacation, kept him on a lifelong tightrope, a state he had great difficulty living without. All of this anxious excitement connected with deception enhanced his subjective sense of reality. Like Abraham's (1925) patient, he seemed compelled to take revenge on those he saw as depending on him by disappointing them and masochistically submitting to their real or imagined rage and punishment. In the transference, this particular pattern also took the form of keeping critically important material out of some sessions in order to pretend he was the kind of "good man" he thought his analyst wanted him to be, only to slip, via one or another parapraxis, into looking like a liar, a thief, a fool. When his compulsive attempts to deceive the analyst were identified and analyzed, this intelligent man was compelled to present himself as a "ninny," a charlatan, caught in the act, even if or *especially if* he had done *absolutely nothing* wrong. Like Abraham's patient, "an overpowering repetition compulsion forced him to make himself an outcast over and over again just when he had become everybody's favorite" (p. 300).

On a number of occasions he engaged in a stereotyped routine of self-aborted petty thievery, pilfering a small inexpensive article at an upscale store when the proprietor's back was turned, then stealthily replacing the purloined article just in the nick of time while barely stifling the impulse to duck, to shield himself from an anticipated blow, and to scream, "I didn't do it!" Although this scenario represents in large measure the enactment of a childhood fantasy, it is also intricately interwoven with fears and fantasies of imposture: to be in such an elegant store itself was not for the likes of him, and his very presence there was a sham. Here is a prime illustration of *feeling* like an impostor.

For Mr. Ingersoll, being a pretentious poseur reinforced his sense of worth even though those pretensions were generally not validated by others as estimable. His worthiness was validated by others in the areas where he was not a poseur but sometimes thought he was (as in his daily work). When he was honestly self-sufficient, he *felt like* an impostor. In fact, his subjective sense of authenticity increased the more shifting and imitative his identifications became, and the more inauthentic and imposturous he felt, the more, by objective standards, he possessed a consolidated, internalized identity. To be a man ("a mensch") threatened him, with its clear oedipal implications. When he was a child, Mr. Ingersoll's mother was more responsive to the "teacher's pet" aspects of him, the false-sounding recitations of banalities he felt she adored, yet she also found contemptible. He, in turn, cultivated and exaggerated this form of wooing, which most people found obnoxious, which he unconsciously knew. One could not help but be impressed with the quality of self- and other mockery in his ostentatiously self-inflating pretentiousness, especially in his two-timing. But inevitably this quality would attract a woman—never a man—who would share his mother's perverse, castrative ambitions for him. Such liaisons meshed with his characterological proclivities in a way that reinforced resistances to working through the masochistically and narcissistically tinged oedipal conflicts. In the analytic situation, he frequently cast his analyst into the role of judge, before whom he had to proclaim his innocence over and over, even when not guilty. He acted as though she were a lie detector, especially when he could not determine himself whether or not he was being deceptive.

DISCUSSION

All of the case examples presented here illustrate a fear of seriousness, commitment, and taking responsibility for personal action under one's own name—either literally or figuratively. The neurotic component in imposture, a component found in all three patients, along with prestructural pathology of the self, can be greatly illuminated by examining Loewald's (1979) views on the latent and unconscious meanings of autonomy and responsibility. He equates developing an authentic sense of identity and experience of oneself as an agent—being nonimposturous—with unconsciously replacing the oedipal rival, that is, with parricide. This is a most useful way of understanding the conflicts about imposture. The parricidal fantasy for these patients is especially strong, and conflicts about authenticity would be one of its byproducts. Schafer's (1976) views about disclaimed action are of similar value here. Loewald's (1979) view of self-responsibility representing, unconsciously, at once a crime and restitution for a crime embodies a notion of compromise formation that seems particularly apt for the conflicts suffered by those who cannot act under their own name, either literally or in the many derivative ways that constitute imposture in the broader, more ubiquitous sense.

In expanding the role of illusion in, among other things, defying the limits set by reality on the pleasure principle, we turn to a consideration of the functions of reality relations, reality testing, and illusion for impostors and the imposturous.

Mr. Green typifies the analysand who can tolerate the analysis, especially the transference, only if it is experienced as not real. There is at the same time a fear of being unmasked as only illusory. The reliance on and the attempted analysis of omnipotent fantasy to the exclusion of reality testing constitute a problem for some patients who had been, previous to their analysis, in illusion-fostering treatments; that is, in treatments that place a premium on role playing or where material and historical reality and objective truths are not of paramount importance. The psychoanalytic method itself, because of its focus on fantasy, may also reinforce illusory self-feelings in those with imposturous tendencies. Such patients find any shifts toward a reality focus, which are particularly important in their analyses, to be damaging to the treatment itself. In the previous, pseudo-analytic therapies, the unreal quality of the role-playing exercises, the experiments, and the participation in innovative modalities that sometimes border on charlatanism all serve the illusory function of safety and surely must accommodate the character anomalies of the imposturous, who become threatened when the nonimposturous aspects of the personality are taken too seriously. These modalities do not require of the patients that they call into question their dependence on make-believe to sustain their subjective sense of integration. A good analysis must encourage these patients to call into question such dependency in order to strike the proper balance between fantasy and reality.

A particular transference paradigm makes analysis of the imposturous extremely difficult. The feelings of inauthenticity these patients seek for their cohesive sense of self-identity are antithetical to the very work required in being an analysand. The search for truth, for authenticity and the reality of the transference, despite its markedly illusory quality, are extraordinarily difficult and often not tolerable for such individuals. The kind of as-if person under consideration has a heightened sense of reality and integration when he or she succeeds in having the imposture believed by others, an outcome certainly contrary to the aims of analysis. As Kohut (1971) points out, some patients quite literally seek out psychic structure in the *mirroring* responses of others. When the analyst's mirroring during the initial phases of treatment consolidates the false self, which includes the false *analytic self*, the imposturous analysand behaves even more for the mirror in the inauthentic way he or she has felt

reflected. It is then extremely difficult to subject that very mirroring to analysis.

Any consideration of the impostor would be incomplete without some recognition of the importance of the audience to the
impostor. As Schrier and Libow (1993) have noted, impostors
are not content to play out their mendacious roles in private.
They must have an audience. Like all deceivers, they feel contempt for the people they deceive and exhilaration whenever the
deceptions are successful. In their study of the Munchausen by
proxy syndrome, they conclude that lying plays two roles for
imposturous patients: it transforms unbearable reality and creates a life in which the extremely egocentric individual can be
the hero. The authors conclude that there are two reasons that
others must necessarily be involved in the impostor's fantasy.
The first is that convincing others intensifies the truth value of
the deception. The second is summarized in a latter-day version
of Fenichel's (1939) incisive understanding of lies: "if people can
be convinced to believe that unreal things are real, then the
obverse may also be true: menacing reality may be unreal"
(p. 125). It is to the end of enhancing the role of illusion in reality
relations that the impostor seeks out the cooperating, colluding
audience that may be hoodwinked.

Abraham (1925) was aware of the twofold importance of the
audience toward whom the impostor consciously or unconsciously directs his performance: its susceptibility to being
taken in by imposturousness and its function in sustaining the
impostor's sense of identity. He notes how the impostor-prisoner
he studied had always been able to gain the confidence of people,
such as prison guards, who would not normally be deceived, only
to betray their confidences. The impostor wishes to dupe and to
be engaging to everyone in order to gain narcissistic satisfaction
from their unending admiration. Then he has to disappoint those
who have come to love him in order to take revenge on them.
To bring these happy conditions to a speedy end partakes of an
overpowering repetition compulsion. A relational or dyadic
perspective is indeed required for a thorough understanding of

the impostor and the audience, as it is for understanding the gullible dyadic relationship between patients who lie (see Chapter 3) and their analysts.

Greenacre (1958a) adds to the repetition compulsion perspective the interpersonal and social significance of a universal wish to be duped by a charmer, a hunger to believe in the fraud. The secret of the impostor's appeal to others lies, as we have stated earlier, in the universal longing to return to that happy state of omnipotence that adults have to relinquish. Greenacre refers particularly to the role of the audience's confirming reaction in giving the impostor a realistic sense of the false self and a heightened subjective sense of integration and reality when he or she succeeds in being believed by others who are taking the place of the idealized, mirroring mother. The lure of participating vicariously in another's illusions, particularly those of omnipotence that one has renounced oneself, accounts for the "fascinating effect of the narcissistic personality" (Olden 1941). This effect tends toward the universal, as even those who consciously give up a belief in omnipotence unconsciously have preserved the belief and seek it in others.

Naturally, some are more susceptible than others to serve as the impostor's audience, and certain impostors are sensitive to whom these individuals might be. Often the motive is not so much to deceive, but, as we have been emphasizing, to achieve validation for one's sense of identity, as imposturously based as that might be.

So, for the noncriminal impostor–"swindler," swindling of admiration or narcissistic supplies is a motive. So is revenge. Finkelstein (1974), in his case presentation of the generally found dyad of gullibility that we are stressing throughout this book, points out that his patient Teddy, in his imposturous seduction of his analyst-audience and others, was identifying with his seductively aggressive mother. An important motive for Teddy, as for Mr. Ingersoll, was to take revenge by making fools of his believing audience and thus discharge some of the repressed hostility he felt toward his mother. Mr. Ingersoll thus

made the representatives of his mother victims of his pathological pretentiousness, a variety of deception, thereby enjoying cas-
trating the vain, controlling, seductive phallic mother with whom
he identified. This case also exemplified the superego lacunae
so typical of imposture, where one or both parents encouraged
and enjoyed, vicariously, the child's omnipotence with which
they identified. Teddy was thus enabled to believe in his own
lies as he identified with his parents' lies about him. At the same
time, he resented their false estimation of him and took revenge
on all audiences, repeating and displacing the revenge he originally wanted to express in the child–parent dyad of deceptions.
In this instance, as in most, imposture is seen as overdetermined,
a symptom, a compromise formation, a character defect with
monumental interpersonal consequences. Apparently other
impostors had parents who showed the same vicarious satisfac-
tions from their child's role playing, the same easy acceptance
of the child's lying, and the same encouragement of imposture,
with predictable interpersonal consequences.

A rather strictly interpersonal view is taken by Gottdeiner
(1982), who sees the impostor as a flatterer who "is able to
weave his way through this interpersonal operation" (p. 445).
McDougall rightly (1980) adds the intrapsychic to the interpersonal perspective in her consideration of a particular version of
a fantasized audience whom she calls the "anonymous spectator." She believes that such an Other is a significant influence
in the fantasies of those who suffer from perversion. It was
essential for the patients she described that this anonymous
Other watch, but equally important that he or she be *duped*. In
keeping with our observations of individuals with imposturous
tendencies, many of whom do indeed suffer from perversions,
the patients she described, like the patient, Mr. Green, described
in this chapter, needed the anonymous spectator, a fantasy
often projected onto the analyst, to be seen as serious; but the
analysis itself must be turned into a game, with all its accomplishments false. For this man, illusions of both infantile
omnipotence and incestuous possibilities could be maintained.

We close with a quotation from Erikson (1959), whose famous work on identity includes an important reference to imposture, referred to earlier in Chapter 1, as a severe identity crisis. It also presumes a *motivational* component in the negative identity of imposture, namely, a hateful repudiation of the most dangerous and yet the most real identifications with the parents at various critical stages of development over the life cycle. In discussing the case of a young American girl of Middle European descent who convincingly constructed for herself and others an imposturous identity as Scottish, Erikson said:

> I went along with the story, implying that it had more inner truth than reality to it. The bit of reality was, as I surmised, the girl's attachment in early childhood to a woman neighbor who had come from the British Isles; the force behind the near-delusional "truth" was the paranoid form of a powerful death wish (latent in all severe identity crises) against her parents. The semi-deliberateness of the delusion was indicated when I finally asked the girl how she managed to marshal all the details of life in Scotland. "Bless you, sir," she said in a pleading Scottish brogue, "I needed a past." [pp. 130–131]

She could have added, "and a present, and a future, too."

5

THE PLIGHT
OF THE SUPERVISOR
WITH THE
IMPOSTUROUS CANDIDATE

Administrators of psychoanalytic training institutes, in charge of deciding whether their candidates or supervisees should progress to completion, are at times more or less taken in by candidates who suffer from imposturous tendencies of one degree or another. Supervisors, progression committees, and others entrusted with assessing the candidates' suitability and readiness to do analytic work may constitute, for the candidate with imposturous tendencies, the audience that inadvertently heightens his or her imposturous ego tendencies. The supervisor serves in the dyad as that "anonymous spectator" who tends to be duped into admiration of the more grandiose defensive aspects of the imposturous deception (McDougall 1980). The supervisor's admiration is essential for the success of the imposture.

Supervisors of psychoanalysis and psychoanalytic therapy are faced with real dilemmas when teaching students with signifi-

Note: This chapter is an expanded version of an article written by Helen K. Gediman, entitled "The Plight of the Imposturous Candidate: Learning amidst the Pressures and Pulls of Power in the Institute," published in *Psychoanalytic Inquiry*, 1986, volume 6, pp. 67–91.

cant imposturous tendencies. In addition to teaching the art and technique of analytic work, they must engage their supervisees in adventures of discovery about the truth of their own psyches as well as those of their patients. Supervisors may unwittingly reinforce a candidate's false self because they are susceptible, as are we all, to identifying unconsciously with the wished-for omnipotence that the imposturous candidate expresses so obviously and ego syntonically (see Gediman 1985a). On the other hand, what has been identified, often after a long-delayed recognition, as a form of pathological imposture may indeed resemble, phenomenologically, the first steps of the *normal* process of learning to become a psychoanalyst. In most cases it is the norm that the beginning candidate feels exposed and inadequate and fears that he or she is not doing vital work: that is, the beginner is narcissistically vulnerable. Supervisors of beginners are not surprised when they observe a certain degree of unintegrated role-playing. Additionally, the neophyte trainee is encouraged to assume, in a controlled and limited sense, multiple identifications with both patients and supervisors in order to develop empathy and analytic wisdom.

Commonly, analysts in training, like the artists to whom Greenacre (1958b) refers, feel and fear that they are impostors, especially at the beginning of their careers. The fact that various selves, or, more exactly, variations on one self are required for analytic work may lead to some of the same fears. That is, the analyst and the artist make changes in self-presentation and self-organization, specific and within the proscribed limits of doing analysis or creative aesthetic work. Among the imposturous, these limits do not hold.

We would hope that, in the candidate in our profession and in the trainee in related disciplines incorporating psychoanalytic psychotherapy, the multiple identifications are temporary and goal related and are not indicative of the poorly integrated identities of those suffering from serious imposturous tendencies. Unfortunately such is not always the case. It is particularly not the case when a candidate who *does suffer* from imposturous tendencies comes up against the real power of the institute. By real power, we refer to the supervisor's responsibility to evaluate the candidate and the institute's power to recommend continuance or termination of training. The power issue comes into all "tilted" relationships (Greenacre 1954). The tilted power structure of the analytic relationship is one in which the analyst can omit— protected by pledges of anonymity and abstinence—but the patient cannot. This inequality parallels the tilted relationship in the supervisory situation, in which the supervisor, having more real power, including the power to omit feedback on certain judgments about the supervisee, provides a setting in which "lying" and omissions would also be a possibility for some supervisees. In supervision, there are actually two tilted relationships, tilted by virtue of the real power invested in the supervisor by both the candidate and the institute. Imposture, in those with significant imposturous tendencies, may be one pathological way of adapting to a real power structure when one's own survival in the institute is dependent on identification with the values, expectations, and roles of the powers that be. In this chapter, we illustrate at some length how the distortions of the tilted reality made by an imposturous supervisee often take the form of shifting, mimicking, poorly integrated identifications, the very kinds of identifications we describe in Chapter 4 as found among the impostor and other kinds of imposturous patients.

A certain degree of role playing in our candidates is expectable and functions as a guide for what the candidate believes is expected of him or her. However, we often miss noticing that this role playing might also suggest both learning and characterological difficulties. When, for example, role playing persists too long—that is, beyond the period during which it is a normal phase of the initial learning process—we should then suspect that we may be dealing with a form of imposture. Such imposturous candidates are often discovered, eventually and, often too belatedly, by supervisors who finally recognize that they have been hoodwinked. When the supervisors report the difficulty, the candidate may be labeled character disordered, even psychopathic, and then dropped from the institute. Indeed, supervisors and administrators of psychoanalytic training institutes bear major responsibility for safeguarding their profession from the dangers to patients and to the public at large that could emanate from therapists suffering from serious degrees of characterological deceptiveness.

Why does it often take so long to recognize such trainees? One reason is that there are various stages in the learning process. Perhaps analysts and supervisors are gullible in certain areas. Perhaps we are too easily conned by our "clones." We embrace our ideal selves when we think we see them in our students, whose ideal is to be like us by acting like us. Such oversights and gullibility in allowing candidates to violate boundaries are prototypical examples of the failure to maintain the two-pronged analytic stance that we have been advocating. We refer again here to the suspension of disbelief coupled with a healthy skepticism, a stance as important for the supervisor as it is for the analyst in detecting deception and ensuring against his or her own gullibility, narcissistic indulgences, and omnipotent enactments. More precisely, when we sense that the candidate's imitativeness is simply a reflection of a fault inevitable in the initial phases of the learning process, it is sufficient to suspend disbelief. However, when we sense imitativeness as reflecting a basic fault of serious characterological pathology of deception, we are well advised to turn to skepticism. Our two-pronged stance mitigates against the supervisor's omnipotent fantasy that these traits are easily modifiable by usual supervisory means, just as it mitigates against the analyst's fantasy of curing severe psychopathology by standard analytic interventions.

As a further complication to the problem of gulling and gullibility in the supervisory situation, issues of real power are important influences in the ascending triadic systems—patient–candidate/analyst–supervisor; candidate/analyst–supervisor–institution—involved in the supervisory situation. In the real world (Freud's "material" reality) as opposed to the intrapsychic world (psychic reality) there is real power.

Real power *presses* on any candidate insofar as the supervisor evaluates his or her progress or will have a say about eventual graduation, or even about referrals, promotions, and degree of success as an eventual peer. Howard Shevrin (in Wallerstein 1981) wrote up his experiences of the effects of real power when he was a candidate being supervised by Herbert Schlesinger. Schlesinger, in turn, was collaborating with others in a supervision study group by writing up his supervisory work with Shevrin. This supervision study group had real power since Schlesinger's write-up was to be part of a book to be published. Shevrin was not informed of these activities, and he learned of them only when the completed manuscript, about to be published, was delivered to him. Feeling prey to a deception, a betrayal of trust by his supervisor and others, he filed legal suit. Eventually, he was invited to write his own chapter for the Wallerstein book, in which he offers his views on why his supervisor described him as emotionally "cool" and as relating with an exaggerated objectivity. Shevrin explains that he adopted this style in part because of his conviction that the institute *expected* a cool, objective approach from him and because of his belief that his evaluation at the institute and at his full-time job depended on it. It was thus only natural for him to emulate his "cool and objective" supervisor. Shevrin is quick to point out how these factors of emulation and identification (which are also typical of the imposturous) do not relate exclusively to resistance and intrapsychic conflict, but also to institutional role conflict and the theoretical commitments embodied in institutional policy. He concludes that the supervisor–teacher should not have real administrative power and believes that unresolved institutional role conflict is a major factor in alienating and infantilizing some supervisees.

In a review of Wallerstein's book, Gediman (1983) notes how real institutional role conflict (material reality) may be drawn into the orbit of intrapsychic conflict and the transferences and countertransferences (psychic reality) of all three participants in triadic systems:

> This possibility would not preclude that institutionally related role conflicts may not have been operating autonomously (i.e., in and of themselves), relatively unrelated to significant unresolved intrapsychic conflict issues of any of the parties involved. One might then have hard evidence that a decision to be secretive [or imitative] in order to be politically wise may be more or less neurotically motivated at the same time as it is an adaptive decision simply to be politically wise. [p. 423]

Shevrin, of course, was not imposturously imitating, but was a good candidate in the initial phases of psychoanalytic training. He was simply acting wisely in adapting to the expectations of the institute. In this instance, and generally speaking, being politic and tactful are adaptive modes of deception.

Learning to be an analyst and learning to be an analysand lend themselves readily both to *feeling* imposturous and, in some instances, to *being* imposturous in troublesome ways. It is important to realize that imposturous tendencies sometimes can be situated in a normal context: developmentally speaking, children imitate before they internalize. This normal process of imitation parallels the normal phase of imitation in the process of learning to do analysis, in which supervisees imitate their training and supervising analysts before they identify with their way of working at a fully integrated level. Sometimes, however, we are justified in suspecting as-if and other imposturous tendencies that do not reflect norms of development and learning. We are alerted to the pathological when candidates report to the supervisor in a manner that seems to be only simple mimicry of an analytic role model, reminiscent of childlike role modeling and patterning of prescribed technique. We are especially alerted to character pathology when candidates undergo kaleidoscopic shifts in what is purportedly analytic behavior and when, in reporting, they enact unreflectively with the supervisor what they believe to be their patient's personality. The candidates delude themselves, as it were, with their own impersonations of an idealized imago of the analyst. These unreflective, imitative enactments, often made in an attempt to adapt to perceived real power, constitute the *pathological parallelisms* par excellence of imposture, phenomena that are included in the illustrative case of Dr. Jenkins to be presented shortly.

Imitation or role playing normally would be a precursor of more consolidated identifications in learning to do analysis. Therefore, only over time and with some difficulty can we draw the line between what is normal and phase-specific imitative learning, on the one hand, and the role-playing and imitativeness of pathological imposture, on the other. In drawing that fine line, it is necessary to show that the disturbances in the sense of reality of the imposturous individual are extreme variations of some important but specifically goal-directed requirements of doing and learning to do analysis. For example, trainees *must* make trial and flexible identifications with their patients. This requirement is more dangerous for some than for others, particularly for those with significant boundary problems whose fundamental reality sense is disturbed precisely by virtue of multiple, shifting identifications, which is one essential process required in conducting an analysis. A therapist *must* empathize with the patient, but if his or her point of contact is exclusively either the patient's primitive unconscious or more superficial peripheral expressions that are easily imitated, then important failures in empathy will ensue. The very fineness of this line makes it difficult to discern and may delay the detection of serious imposture for a long time, even in the very best of institute settings.

An additional problem is the ubiquity of as-if states, which are arranged on a spectrum ranging from the transitory to the stabilized. Thus, some degree of imposture is to be found among the normal as well as among the characterologically imposturous. Since a consolidated professional identity does not develop until late in the learning process, early detection of imposture is understandably difficult except in blatantly pathological, especially psychopathic cases. One might pose the question of differentiating the normal from the pathological as follows. Will the supervisor's conveyance or demonstration of the analytic approach, which ideally should parallel or reflect the *essence* and not the superficial "technology" of the analytic process, lead to deep, consolidated, flexible identifications, or will it lead only to mere shallow imitations? The imposturous candidate is indeed an extreme example of failed identification with the analyst's fundamental way of working. Although it is hoped that the situation is very rare, a contaminating influence might be discerned when the candidate imitates his or her training analyst who might in fact be conducting the candidate's analysis with significant inauthenticity. There are, however, many in-between situations in which problems result from various real faulty teaching and learning situations, the consequences of which may not be too easy to distinguish from the characterological problems of the candidate. It is here that the designations made by the COPE Study Group of "dumb spots" (difficulties due to learning problems or inexperience) and "blind spots" (characterological or countertransference difficulties) are relevant.

It has been said that knowledge of the gospel is not sufficient to preach well and honestly. Similarly, knowledge of technique, gleaned from books and lectures, is not sufficient for being an authentic analyst. Fred Wolkenfeld (personal communication to Helen K. Gediman, 1985) suggests the gospel analogy for understanding an aspect of this important relationship between imitation and reportorial honesty in the psychoanalytic learning process. To carry through the analogy of the clergy's use of the self in the transmission of religion and spirituality to the use of the self in the psychoanalytic learning situation, knowledge of the "analytic gospel" alone is insufficient to perform the essential process of doing adequate analysis. This unique requirement of our work has been called by many names: internalizations, identifications, transformations of the self into the cohesive analytic self, or the development of the candidate's potential as an analyzing instrument. Ironically, a student's attempt to present to a supervisor the gospel truth of his or her sessions with a patient, even though really encouraged by some supervisors, could be fundamentally dishonest—as is seen in the illustrative case of Dr. Jenkins.

The reality of candidates being required to work with several supervisors who work differently from one another can also stimulate imposturous tendencies. Although such individual differences in styles and ways of working are to be found even in the most theoretically homogeneous of training settings, they are particularly marked in institutes that offer diversity in pluralistic and multimodal theoretical orientations and that encourage interdisciplinary crossing back and forth. Working effectively with a multiplicity of theoretical axes requires an ability to shift adroitly from one perspective to another. This requirement of oscillating between one vantage point and another could potentiate latent imposturous tendencies of fluidity and facileness in candidates predisposed in that direction.

Another characteristic of training that is also conducive to imposture among the vulnerable is to be found in those aspects of the supervisory process that involve rapport, engagement, and mutual give-and-take between supervisor and candidate. The supervisor's authentic positive input, feedback, and validation sustain and enhance the subjective sense of integrity and cohesiveness of supervisees. Those with imposturous identifications may thrive more on the feedback of an audience than do the nonimposturous. The requisite *positive climate*, however, may hold serious *masking potential* for imposture. Greenacre (1958a,b) notes that the false self becomes reflected back, magnified, and strengthened with such mirroring affirmation. Therefore, supervisory situations in which there is good rapport, comfort, and engagement may benefit the self-experience of the average-expectable candidate in average-expectable ways, but could have the unfortunate effect of impeding the detection of possible imposturousness for a long time.

ILLUSTRATIVE CASE MATERIAL

The data presented here are not psychoanalytic. That is, they derive from process notes of a supervisory and not a psychoanalytic or psychotherapeutic relationship. Therefore, references regarding pathology, including those implying fragmented identifications and difficulty in distinguishing self from object and object from object, may not be as reliable as those deriving from the psychoanalytic situation.

Dr. Jenkins

For reasons of confidentiality, this case illustration deals with a supervisee in psychoanalytic psychotherapy who was not and never has, to our knowledge, become a candidate at a psychoanalytic institute. Since there are continuities between the learning process during supervision of psychoanalytic therapy and that of psychoanalysis proper, this case is considered to be an apt example.

This supervisory case material places particular emphasis on disturbances in the sense of reality and the ways in which these disturbances differ from the average-expectable, phase-acceptable learning processes. The supervisee, Dr. Jenkins, manifested hypertrophied and limited empathy and other disturbances in the sense of reality. This case of imposture typified, par excellence, a *pathological parallelism*, in which personal problems with multiple, shifting identifications lead to a deficient understanding of the treatment process. The work with the patient was repeated or enacted in parallel fashion in supervision. This pathological parallelism, when found in a supervisee with the vulnerabilities under scrutiny here, must be regarded *in part* as a result of the experience of powerlessness and fragility that the supervisee with imposturous tendencies inevitably feels in a training institute.

This kind of enactment is but one form of parallel process, defined (Gediman and Wolkenfeld 1980, Wolkenfeld 1990) as a multidirectional representational system in which major psychic events, including complex behavioral patterns, affects, and conflicts, occurring in one dyadic situation—analysis or supervision—are repeated in the other. A nonpathological parallelism, then, could also reflect multiple, shifting identifications, which are nonproblematic and remain within the limits of the requirements of doing analytic work. In keeping with our main thesis, then, issues of powerlessness and fragility would not emerge as importantly in these average-expectable parallelisms as they do in the pathological parallelisms found among supervisees such as Dr. Jenkins, who suffer from significant imposturous tendencies.

Although this case material focuses on problems with imposture, it is important to keep in mind throughout the corollary issue of *power impact*. Power impact refers to the fact that the supervisee understands that the supervisor evaluates the supervisee's progress and has real power in deciding his or her fate in the field. As we noted earlier in the case of Howard Shevrin, trying to impress the supervisor might be a form of white lie in the nonimposturous, or of as-if or psychopathic tendencies in the imposturous, those whom we have described as particularly vulnerable to eruptions of characterological disturbances under the impact of real power. Power impact, then, is always suggested and is always a significant though sometimes latent motivating force underlying Dr. Jenkins's difficulties in supervision. The supervisor is, after all, not simply a teacher, but an evaluator and a critically determining influence on the student's future as well. Dr. Jenkins is not representative of the more average-expectable degrees of imposture, such as those inherent in the tactful and adaptive white lies of the initial learning stages that fall at the normative end of the spectrum, as part of the psychopathology of everyday life. Her responses in supervision illustrate a conglomerate of fairly extreme imposturous tendencies. It would be heuristically valuable to compare that extreme degree of imposture with the average-expectable degree of as-if-ness that is inherent in the early stages of the psychoanalytic learning process.

Dr. Jenkins illustrates hypertrophied empathy-like responses (see Khron 1974) as well as the prototypically imposturous trends common among those who have difficulties establishing firm ego boundaries that enable a strong personal center of gravity or orientation. As a supervisee she was notably compliant to the letter with all that her supervisor asked of her, but she had great difficulty in grasping the spirit of the enterprise. She had originally taken verbatim notes and read them during supervisory sessions. The resulting material had a lifeless, distant, isolated quality. As a corrective and in an attempt to get her to loosen up, her supervisor suggested that she take minimal process notes, hoping that she could then focus more on interacting with her. Dr. Jenkins followed that suggestion by producing masses of noncohesive material that she "extemporaneously" reported. When the supervisor was troubled enough to comment to her about the inauthentic sound of the material presented in this way, Dr. Jenkins revealed that she had still taken six or seven pages of verbatim notes, as lengthy as ever, but, as she explained, since the supervisor did not want her to read them in the sessions, she had read them over assiduously in advance of the supervisory session and had been conscientiously repeating them from memory. She revealed this with no apparent insight into the absurdity of her actions. By committing her verbatim notes to memory and then reporting what she remembered, she was acting as if she were spontaneous while in fact she was more stimulus-bound than ever. Whatever characterological problems contributed to this style, an intense anxiety to placate the powers that be was also operative. She was in fact behaving like a caricature of an analyst. Although imposturous caricatures often contain a degree of mockery of and therefore a sadistically perverse masquerade and an aggressive attack on the analyst–supervisor's sense of reality, this motive did not seem to feature prominently in Dr. Jenkins's presentation. It certainly does not feature prominently in the beginner, the simply inept, or in the nonimposturous who are difficult to teach.

Despite her blind and/or dumb spots, Dr. Jenkins seemed to catch on extraordinarily quickly to the drift of the supervisor's questions and hunches concerning the patient, and she confirmed all too readily any psychodynamic hunches that she discerned lay behind the questions. She never, however, spontaneously introduced any hunches of her own. The problem that aroused her supervisor's suspicions was that she started to report as verbatim material something that immediately confirmed the supervisor's speculative hypothesis, as though it had naturally followed at just that point in the memorized notes of the session at which she had intervened. Dr. Jenkins appeared to finish the supervisor's very sentences as soon as the supervisor introduced the thought that began them. Instead of developing her own center of gravity in directing her work as a therapist and as a supervisee, she was excessively attentive to the expectations of others, consequently displaying an excess of misdirected and superficial empathy toward what she thought her supervisor was asking for. This is, of course, a special use of the term "empathy," referring not to the exquisite attunements of one with the other that the word ordinarily connotes but more to what Khron (1974) describes as borderline empathy—hypertrophied, unprocessed, unintegrated identifications found not only among those with borderline personality disorders but also in a variety of others suffering from disturbances in core identity. This particular supervisee acted as though the supervisor adhered to a doctrine to which she must adapt, unselectively, in order to fulfill her requirement.

This prototypically imposturous supervisee had a shifty way of reporting allegedly verbatim material that was reminiscent of certain borderline or hysterical patients who lapse into pseudologia fantastica when they become involved in conveying their experience to another person. Dr. Jenkins repeatedly "replayed," in a vivid way, a conversation that had taken place between her patient and his friend. It was as though she had been exactly in the place in which that conversation had occurred and never in the place—her consulting room—in which the patient had reported the conversation to her. That is, she and the interaction between herself and her own patient, and her emotional-cognitive responses to him, were simply not present in the material she reported in supervision. Her point of orientation, or center of gravity, seemed now to be located too empathically in the place in which the original extra-analytic event occurred. She reported conversations that she had never herself heard with such uncannily sounding accuracy that the supervisor began to suspect that these elaborated interchanges were largely the products of her imagination.

When such a supervisee enacts what the patient was saying about a friend, or gives a nearly verbatim account of what a friend told the patient or what the patient told his friend, *but from the friend's point of view*, there is too much positioning "inside the friend's head." This positioning leaves out entirely what might have been happening in the therapy itself with respect to the ways the patient was talking, associating, and relating or to the ways the supervisee as therapist was listening and engaged in interaction with the patient.

To some, such a supervisee surely might appear to be behaving in a psychopathic manner, but is this really so? She might be described as shifty, not in the more psychopathic sense of being evasive or of producing fudged or made-up process material, but of presenting material that reflected her nonsolidity and nonrootedness with respect to her poor center of gravity and too permeable ego boundaries. She conveyed no sense of what actually transpired between her patient and herself in a way that was consistent with the style of her contact with her supervisor, which was limited to reading or presenting verbatim notes from memory. When the problem was called to her attention, she said that she was doing the kind of "experiential reporting" she had been taught by former supervisors. Here, too, it sounded as though she were imitating what she thought experiential reporting should be without at all understanding its spirit or purpose.

Two problems plaguing the supervisor were *whose* experience was being reported and *what kind* of notes were these where the patient's extra-analytic interactions with significant others were reported with such suspiciously vivid detail.

To check out her hunch, which had become a conviction that she was dealing with an as-if supervisee with significant imposturous tendencies, the supervisor decided to introduce a new teaching strategy in which mirroring and feedback were largely withheld. This decision to be more silent, laid back, opaque, and nonengaging—closer to the role an analyst would assume—was made because this supervision definitely appeared to be an instance in which input, validation, and feedback were helping consolidate imposturous, inauthentic identifications. Furthermore, since a more pathological, hypertrophied, empathic attunement is highly selective in areas relevant to narcissistic gratification, the fluency of its expression is prone to slippage into arbitrary fluidity once the supervisor in the dyad does not offer enough cues as to how well the supervisee is doing or what is expected. As we have said, what is expected has real consequences for survival in the institute, and this power impact can reinforce pre-existing imposturous tendencies. If supervisory mirroring or the gleam in the supervisor's eye is withheld, something we generally are not inclined to do in a comfortable, collaborative supervisory alliance, and if the supervisor is laid back, opaque, refraining from engaging in mutual but potentially cuing-in exchanges, the imposturous supervisee may shift from as-if reporting of sessions into more disjointed and confused communications. After having altered her style, the supervisor was then confronted with the same kind of difficulties reported in Chapter 4 regarding Anais Nin's Sabina and her relationship with the "lie detector." Like Sabina, Dr. Jenkins sounded glib, disjointed, fluid, confused, discontinuous, and garbled. Like Nin's lie detector character, the supervisor was confused by the many contradictions and confusions and by the lack of cohesiveness in the candidate's reporting.

When the supervisor actually remained silent for an entire

session, she could hardly discern any meaning in the material Dr. Jenkins was reporting. Like Nin's Sabina, the supervisee's incoherent, shifty, ramblings were apparently going downhill from the mere imposturous to the more psychopathic state of conscious and deliberate lies. There was nothing in what the supervisor heard from Dr. Jenkins's report that she could identify as authentic, that is, as something that one would reasonably expect to transpire between a therapist and a patient. Little held together cohesively, consistently, or systematically in the manner of any psychoanalytic reporting or process or that would be recognized as such by analysts in general. It was clear that a regression had occurred in the supervisee in response to the supervisor's less interactive style. Dr. Jenkins's response to this shift in stance, posture, and attitude made the analyst wonder how she was responding in her personal analysis to a similar anonymous and abstinent stance on her analyst's part. Presumably, she was regressing in a similar way in her analysis.

The supervisory situation is not a therapeutic one, even though the supervisor, in this instance, shifted her stance by becoming less interactive and that stance was more typical of an analyst than a supervisor. Although there is some similarity between the supervisory and the analytic stance, usually anonymity and abstinence on the part of the supervisor do not and should not promote regression in the same way that they do in psychoanalytic treatment. Regressions occur in analysis even among neurotic and reasonably normal analysands. That does not usually happen in supervision, even when the supervisor conducts the process for greater or lesser periods of time in a relatively noninteractive way. It became apparent that Dr. Jenkins's role playing at what she believed was expected of her became all the more hollow, false, and inauthentic when the supervisor no longer provided a scaffolding, when she was no longer the colluding audience unwittingly taken in by her sham stereotypes and caricatures of analytic activity. When the supervisee finally was confronted with this difficulty, she sounded bewildered, stressed, and slightly angry. Now there was "trouble in paradise," in contrast to the previous apparent harmony, which looked retrospectively like sham interaction and sham rapport. At most, Dr. Jenkins could sound like a child imitating what she thought she should sound like in the role of an adult analyst delivering an "objective" interpretation.

Generally speaking, supervisors in this situation, upon discovering that they have been deceived, often have strong emotional reactions to the deception. The feelings induced, whether of shame, anger, or outrage, may be mitigated when they can be understood as induced by a nontalented as-if supervisee. These feelings, referred to recently as "supertransference" (Teitelbaum 1990), must be mastered just as an analyst's countertransference is mitigated and mastered. However, supervision is not analysis, and the supervisor must be concerned with the learning problems rather than with the blind spots, which are the training analyst's and not the supervisor's job to deal with.

We expect role playing and imitation in the early stages of psychoanalytic education for most of our supervisees, including the very talented. But when this imitative phase persists long past its due, we are dealing with serious pathology and not simply with a normal phase in the learning process. After all, it was not until well into their work that this supervisor realized role playing seemed to be mostly all that Dr. Jenkins could do. She was not progressing toward a consolidated identity as an analytic therapist, and she must have sensed, whether consciously or unconsciously, her inability to do so. Nonetheless, the supervisor persisted, without yet realizing that her very persistence was an exercise of real power that only increased her vulnerable trainee's bewilderment and deep anxieties. The supervisor's emotional reactions, or induced "supertransference" feelings, can serve as a signal that one is dealing with imposture or with deceit in one or more of its other forms and not with the anxiety that is typical of an early learning phase. Such feelings should signal supervisors to temper their zeal to teach and to impart, analogous to the analyst' s wish to cure. The narcissistic balance will be restored and, along with it, the requisite balance between the suspension of disbelief and healthy skepticism.

After the supervisor decided, as a corrective, to be more opaque, and after she had confronted Dr. Jenkins with her problem in developing her own center of gravity in her experiential reporting, the two no longer engaged in the pseudo-mutuality and give and take that had felt so rewarding to both for approximately a year. The supervisor ceased mirroring her student's responses, which were informed by a vast but superficial and eclectic knowledge of many points of view to which she had been exposed during the course of her training but in which her breadth of knowledge surely exceeded her depth of grasp. As the supervisor began to be convinced of the lack of depth in her supervisee's grasp of the knowledge she was trying in vain to assimilate, she also had an increasingly difficult time reading or getting a handle on what was happening with the patient. This difficulty was due to the supervisor's increased awareness of Dr. Jenkins' difficulties that emerged when the supervisor became more silent so as to not inadvertently cue her in. It was also due to the supervisee's increasingly evident lapses into fragmented, disconnected, and now more obviously "inauthentic" reporting. She confronted her student with this difficulty, suggesting once again that she stop trying to take or to memorize any detailed process notes but to come in simply with an outline that she could fill in from memory. She also explicitly told her that she would just listen for a while, for she was concerned that their interactions themselves were biasing her student's mode of reporting.

The supervisee then came with no notes at all. She made obvious gestures of searching diligently the back of her memory for what had happened in the session. She engaged in as-if reporting that, without the supervisor's cues, sounded very incoherent and impossible to follow, confirming the hunch about the conditions under which hypertrophied but selective empathy-like responsiveness *fails*. The supervisee, too, noticed her increasing incoherence and actually proposed that she was having difficulties empathizing and therefore reporting accurately because her *patient* was a slippery as-if personality and that was a very difficult thing for her to convey accurately in supervisory sessions! Clearly, she suffered boundary confusion, projecting some endopsychic perception of herself perhaps into her patient.

Was this trainee an impostor? She did not literally pretend under the cover of someone else's name. But she did something very much like that. She pretended under the cover of someone else's *style* and *role*. She was *masquerading* herself, psychologically speaking, as a version of a psychoanalytic therapist that was not very well internalized, but that corresponded to her reading of the expectations and pressures of the training institution. A certain sort of masquerade in this case is normative because it is a requirement of the learning task in its beginning phases. Regarding the masquerade as normal in context, then, adds an air of respectability to certain aspects of deception. And because it is normal as a phase of the learning process, the plight of the supervisor–teacher in distinguishing imposturous tendencies from normal learning processes is correspondingly increased, paradoxically, because of the conformity of the deception to the rules of the game. At its most normative, it may be considered part of the psychopathology of everyday life.

The question now facing us is, how was this masquerader similar to and how did she differ from *any* student in the beginning phases of learning, phases that should lead to the optimal use of oneself as an analyzing instrument. Even if we accept Deutsch's (1955) view that imposturous tendencies may be found in all human beings and that the average-expectable case differs only in degree from the pathologically imposturous, it is still essential to capture the very nature, the quality of that difference, in order to distinguish the seriously pathological from the psychopathology of everyday life. This is a major question to be asked not only with respect to the subject matter of this chapter, but throughout this book.

First, Dr. Jenkins's mode of reporting was atypical. Her manner of trying to convey experiential data could be regarded as

imposturous in the artifice of her straining for phenomenologi-
cal accuracy and in the obvious inauthenticity in her way of
producing memorized "process notes." She was also imposturous
in her technique. She fancied herself as making interpretations
whenever she made a verbal statement of any kind to her patient.
Asked why she had called a particular intervention an interpretation, she became imposturous at theorizing: "It was an interpretation because it dealt with the unconscious." Now, none of
this may look like a gross deviation, for we might expect such
loose approximations from any beginner, particularly a very
anxious one. But in context she was glib enough to strongly
suggest imposture. She knew just enough about experiential
reporting; she knew just enough about psychoanalytic theories.
The giveaway was that she knew just enough about *many* theories, some of which were intrinsically incompatible with or contradictory to each other, but whose potentially vexing ambiguities did not seem to raise any question for her as they would for
most thoughtful students. She could shift easily from one to
another frame of reference, embracing all, and was suspiciously
untroubled by theoretical incompatibilities. This propensity for
an easy eclecticism embodied more anarchy than flexibility, and
it suggested a miscarrying of the requisite personal flexibility and
multiple viewpoints essential for doing analytic work. She knew
just enough about technique, but it did not seem to matter to
her if she functioned correctly or incorrectly. And she showed
none of the expectable anxiety of a beginner making mistakes.
She thought she was doing what she was supposed to do.

Dr. Jenkins, then, is not like our more usual nonimposturous
beginners for whom distinctions matter and who learn about
them either receptively or by actively questioning what they are
doing and why, who challenge the supervisor, who do not catch
on right away, and who call *themselves* into question. Interest-
ingly, some of these nonimposturous students frequently *feel*
imposturous in the beginning phases of training and will tell us
that they do. The better integrated neophytes are not so fearful
to question, within acceptable limits, the power of authority and

do so by using their own powers of intelligence and discrimination. Dr. Jenkins, in contrast, unquestioningly accepted everything as though to get on and over with a charade required for the completion of training requirements. The pervasiveness of her shiftiness, the blatantly false quality of her presentation once her supervisor abandoned an encouraging stance in favor of a truly opaque one, revealed a fundamental imposturousness with disturbances in the sense of reality of the self and the world. The imposturous stance might, as LaFarge (1994) notes so well, have shifted here, defensively, into a psychopathic one, as the imposturous grandiosity was no longer mirrored by the other in the gullible dyad. That is, the once gullible Other was no longer gullible, having realized that she was being duped. Once psychopathy enters the picture, defensively or not, there is an aggressive assault on the supervisor's sense of reality. This assault increases the supervisor's plight, just as it adds to the typical countertransferences of analysts treating patients who consciously and deliberately deceive them.

At this point we interrupt the case illustration in order to elaborate two issues. The first, what really happened in the analytic hour, is subsumed under the topic of daydreams in common. The second concerns pathological parallelisms in the treatment and supervisory settings. The case illustration, to repeat, comes from the supervision of psychoanalytic psychotherapy and not psychoanalysis proper, but can be generalized to the supervision of the analytic situation proper.

Daydreams in Common

What really happened in the analytic hour must be reconstructed from more or less ambiguous reports presented by the analyst or the analyst-in-training (we are talking of the supervisory situation now). The nature of psychic reality and of material reality, of "objective truth value" and, in particular, of how knowable one person's psychic reality is to another person is central to the problem of imposture. These issues are also central to all teaching and learning of psychoanalysis, but the particular character problems of Dr. Jenkins illustrate the importance of psychic reality in a unique way. The supervisor never really knows what actually transpired, but has "daydreams in common" (Arlow 1969a,b, Freud 1907) with the patient and the therapist in a way that holds together according to certain more or less specifiable criteria. Sometimes we can only imagine or fantasize what happened. The built-in aesthetic ambiguity of our work situation lends itself so easily to crossing the line between the imaginative and empathic, on the one hand, and between the fantastic and—this is an emphasis that is new—crossing the line into the imposturous, on the other. Here we are touching on *psychic reality*, which is recognizable and apprehendable, provided that the one who is attempting to convey it has access to it, as the imposturous reporter does not. Dr. Jenkins, instead, focused on a particular version of objective reality or objective truth value. That is, her various accounts of her patient's sessions were inconsistent, discontinuous, and oversimplified representations of other people that she could not piece into analytically meaningful patterns. Not only did Dr. Jenkins's reports not hang together in a psychoanalytically meaningful way but they also defied conventional common sense and conventions of coherence. And most important, there was little evidence for their correspondence to anything recognizable that one usually expects to be going on in the analytic situation, mainly because Dr. Jenkins's process reporting did not contain any graspable account of that situation.

In Dr. Jenkins's process reports, we would expect to detect the presence of material that one regularly hears if an analysis is indeed being conducted, assuming a reasonably well-selected patient: evidence of infantile sexuality and aggression; indications of recognizable defense measures; manifestations of anxiety, shame, guilt, and depression; symbolic and other representations of significant body zones and modes; accounts of self-feeling and self-esteem; accounts of oneness and separateness; and certain other themes. If we never hear these motifs in a sustained, coherent way in a candidate's report, we may safely assume that he or she has not grasped them or picked them up and helped the patient develop them. And if the candidate still presents process notes as though he or she were unquestionably doing analysis, we must question the authenticity of the work, just as we do when criteria of objective truth value are not met. What Dr. Jenkins was doing was the very best that she could, but in a fundamentally powerless way, to conform to what she believed the formally institutionalized power structure expected of her. She manifested a lack of elasticity, a deficit in ego strength that left her powerless and contributed to her supervisor's bewilderment, for supervisors understandably do not wish their charges to show ego pathology! It can seem like an offense to the supervisor's wish to maintain the highest standards for the profession and to protect the patients and the public that his trainees are to serve. Supervisors' wishes for unimpaired candidates, however, bespeak pride and narcissistic gratifications in having their students attain the same analytic ideals they hold out for themselves. That narcissistic balance can become skewed for periods of time by denial of a poor candidate's ego pathology, which is manifested in a failure to encourage the trainee to turn to another career and in a failure to use power properly by reporting the pathology appropriately within the institute. We are not obliged to maintain confidentiality in the same way when we function as supervisors as when we function as training analysts. If supervisors are to fulfill their institutionally sanctioned responsibility for making recommendations regarding a candidate's progression, reporting ego pathology should not be regarded as a breach of confidentiality. To the contrary, by not reporting it, the supervisor is engaging in a deception directed toward the candidate, the institute, and the community at large.

Returning to the case of Dr. Jenkins brings us to the second issue to be elaborated: certain *pathological parallelisms* found among the imposturous.

Pathological Parallelisms in Imposture

One of the reasons that even a mild degree of imposture in reporting yields pathological parallelisms par excellence is that the requirements of doing analysis and the criteria for imposture, despite their significant and critical differences, overlap sufficiently to encourage the phenomenon to emerge. This follows the line of thinking adopted by Gediman and Wolkenfeld (1980), according to which the structural and dynamic similarities between psychoanalysis (or psychoanalytic psychotherapy) and supervision guarantee the emergence of parallelisms in the supervisory or learning situation. Those similarities, which now seem relevant to the issue of imposture, center on the requirement of multiple empathic identificatory processes and on the use of the self as an analyzing instrument.

The disturbances in the sense of reality of the self that are hallmark signs of imposture all involve some changes in self-organization and self-presentation. And so does being an analyst involve such changes. However, a most important qualification should be underscored in articulating the differences between imposture and learning to be an analyst: the analyst makes changes in self-organization and self-representation *specific* to the immediate problems of the work and of the analytic situation. The changes in self-organization made by the imposturous supervisee that lead to the pathological parallelisms are general and not subject to consciously deliberate choice and situational requirements. That empathy, multiple shifting identifications, and multiple selves are required for both analytic work and for imposture (the normative aspects of the process, relevant to the psychopathology of everyday life) does not mean that the important differences should be ignored, for they are central to an understanding and possible remediation of the pathological parallelism.

Dr. Jenkins was beginning to describe her *patient* in the very terms the supervisor would have used to describe *her*, a parallel process that contained a pathological parallelism. She told her supervisor how her patient was one of those very slippery people whose identifications were so shallow and fluid that it was very difficult for her to grasp his experience and to report it accurately. She explained that *his* identifications were very unintegrated and he must be an as-if personality. She confessed that when she was relatively quiet, she had trouble following the drift of what he was saying. Now, for the first time, she began to report problematic interactions between herself and her patient, following the occasion when similar problems were addressed in the supervisory interaction! She thought the patient's slipperiness must account for the supervisor's expressed difficulty in following the drift of her material. All told, she acted like someone powerlessly cornered and flailing at making use of poorly understood notions that the supervisor, in her view, was imposing on her. That was her way of surviving. But the supervisor did not see that aspect of her difficulties at the time of her work with the supervisee, for the issue of imposture was then more manifestly palpable than that of power.

Some additional problems emerged around the time that the supervisor was checking out her hunches by refraining from cueing in the supervisee to what she was thinking. Dr. Jenkins reported that her patient had begun to scrutinize her face and her voice for signs of the "correctness" of his own interpretations of his dreams and other material, and for the moral correctness of certain of the behaviors that he was reporting to her. She believed that her patient saw her as fluidly shifting her views of him, and that is why, she said, he needed to scrutinize her so carefully. He then, she asserted, began to comply with one after the other of these shifting projected identifications, which he experienced as coming from her.

In this uncanny parallelism, Dr. Jenkins's description of her patient was suspiciously close to how her supervisor perceived her in the supervisory situation. Most important, this reported view of her patient's dynamics *followed* the supervisor's attempt to convey to her how she was intent on demonstrating her ver-

sion of varied and ever-changing theoretical and technical vir-
tuosity because she expected that her supervisor wished to see
her do that. The problem was that her attempts to comply
resulted in the looseness and fluidity already described. No doubt
both wished to understand: the supervisor her work and the
supervisee her patient. The parallel pressure to know, required
for daydreams in common to yield a meaningful discourse in a
supervisory context, can also yield the pathological or derailed
parallelism of the instance described. The process is considered
derailed because the supervisee presented her patient in the very
way that the supervisor understood the supervisee, but without
consciously realizing that she was doing that. It was as though
she understood much, unconsciously, but could not, for reasons
relevant to the fragmented identity problems of the imposturous,
regard herself as the object of what she understood—projecting,
instead onto her patient.

The pathological parallelism just described reflects a projective identification: the supervisee describes the patient in terms
that actually describe herself, and her manner of describing
constitutes an enactment of the way her supervisor actually
perceived *her*. Such a parallelism constitutes an extreme and
particular example of parallel process as defined earlier—the
repetition in one dyadic situation, either psychotherapy or supervision, of psychic events occurring in the other dyadic situation
of the triad. In observing this parallelism involving projective
identification, the *fluidity of perspective and the multiple viewpoints
required in doing analysis and in learning to do it* might provide
the situational pull for the emergence of the supervisee's as-if
behavior, shared by or at least projected onto her patient as well.

In a later supervisory session—which illustrates a different
but somewhat related point regarding parallelisms—the supervisor shared with Dr. Jenkins a speculative hunch that her patient
favored the circumventions of ordinary obstacles to his goals and
gratifications and that this proclivity was reflected in his con-
tinual use of the "back door" metaphor in dreams and fantasies.
The supervisor conjectured that this metaphor reflected his con-

cerns with his multiple successes at circumventing oedipal prohibitions. The patient, for example, was having an affair with
his supervisor, a married, somewhat older woman, in his on-the-
job training placement. He also believed that when his psychotherapy was terminated he would be able to have a love affair
with the therapist. In the next supervisory session, Dr. Jenkins
rather glibly reported that her patient *told her* how he notices
that he uses the "back door" metaphors to express the way in
which he circumvents ordinary obstacles. He said this metaphor
reflected how he believed he could have possessed his mother
and now believed he could possess the therapist. Dr. Jenkins was
asked how she thought her patient's understanding of this
dynamic formulation evolved in the treatment situation. The
supervisor carefully avoided any reference to the fact that the
patient's apparent discovery was couched in the very terms that
the supervisor herself had explicitly offered speculatively in their
previous supervisory session. Dr. Jenkins became flustered and,
as usual, seemed unable to provide any pertinent sequential data.
Then, as though she had empathically caught on to what was
on her supervisor's mind, she reversed what she had presented
in her initial version and implied that she had interpreted it to
him in a previous session but she forgot which one, and she had
neglected to report that fact. Once again, it was difficult to as-
certain this supervisee's center of gravity or whose experience
she was reporting. She seemed utterly confused herself and
showed no sign of recollecting any actual event in which either
she or her patient had "interpreted" what was *the supervisor's*
speculative hunch.

In a much later session, Dr. Jenkins said she found her patient
engaged in a "psychological lie." Although there may be many
reasons for her reporting this, in context it seems to be yet another pathological parallelism. Although the supervisor never
shared with her any hunches about her artifice in reporting, her
account was in keeping with her characteristic empathic-like
sensitivity in selected areas and suggested that unconsciously,
she may have divined her supervisor's suspicions. Specifically,

the lie, or actually distortion, to which she referred had to do with her patient's reporting to her that upon completing one phase of his on-the-job training, his supervisor had seduced him sexually, when it seemed in fact to Dr. Jenkins that it was the other way around. She then went on to describe her patient as having borderline boundary problems. She also wondered how it was possible for a patient with such serious pathology to receive A-ratings for job performance and even be offered promotions, and concluded that it must have been due to a joking connection the patient himself had made previously with what he called his many A's for "ambition and adulterous achievement." Dr. Jenkins felt certain that anyone who prevaricated so much must have job-training problems as well.

Here was more evidence of the pathological parallelism that in this instance barely disguised the supervisee's lie. It seems evident that Dr. Jenkins had a serious characterological problem area of which she was apparently unaware (a blind spot) and that *also constituted a learning problem for her* (a dumb spot). This difficulty emerged in her report as a parallel difficulty in her patient, the implications of which she only partially understood.

It is precisely this sort of parallelism that constitutes the prototypical example of the parallel impasse requiring a certain kind of supervisory intervention. It is what Gediman and Wolkenfeld (1980) have referred to as the "by-pass." In several recent personal communications, Wolkenfeld and Gediman (1985) have formulated the bypass as that supervisory intervention in which the supervisor addresses the problem indirectly, in a way analogous to an analyst offering a *"deflected transference" interpretation*: the parallelism is discussed as a problem for the patient, but not discussed as a problem for the supervisee. The supervisory bypass, then, avoids the here-and-now supervisory interaction and focuses only on parallel dynamic problems for the patient alone.

Nevertheless, the emergence of such a parallelism can be read as a sign that the supervisee may know unconsciously that he or she has had problems similar to the patient's and would like the benefit of the supervisor's wisdom. Tact, too, would dictate that remarks regarding, in this instance, imposture, boundary confusion, and identity disturbance be addressed in the extra-supervisory sphere, that is, be directed toward the patient's obvious difficulties, rather than to the supervisee's pathology. The parallelism could be discussed more explicitly when it is less obvious or delicate to confront than this supervisee's proclivity toward introjection and projection, or when *more* is really at stake, such as a candidate's suitability to be an analyst. In the case of Dr. Jenkins, it was sufficient, at first, to indicate that her difficulties in dealing with patients' problems in this area might be something she would want to discuss in her personal analysis.

With these principles in mind, the supervisor questioned whether the patient truly had engaged in a lie, suggesting to the supervisee that the patient was probably genuinely confused as to whether he had been led on by a woman in a position of authority and real power or whether he himself was the more seductive one. She also suggested that such confusion probably emerged in the transference as well, in his having a conviction that his therapist was encouraging him to believe in the possibility of a consummated love affair once he was "graduated" upon termination. The supervisor dealt with the additional parallelism of the supervisee's bewilderment about her patient's getting A's and being accepted for advanced career training by bypassing any explicit reference to the possibility that the supervisee might have similar concerns about her supervisor evaluating her work so that she could advance professionally. That is, the supervisor's remarks were limited to an understanding of the patient only. She reminded the supervisee that her patient was working in a very rarefied, esoteric area of specialization, where such boundary slippage not only could go undetected but could be encouraged and rewarded. It was also clear from many things she had said that the patient was quite tuned in to issues of innocence and corruptibility in others and that he exercised considerable charm with people for whom these were problems. The supervisor assumed that, at least unconsciously, Dr. Jenkins "heard" these references as being relevant to herself as well.

In the final supervision sessions, a parallelism emerged that·
was handled not by a bypass, or by addressing its significance
for the patient alone, but by discussing it directly and explicitly
as a parallelism with the supervisee. *Lest we forget the supervisor's*
very real contribution to parallel process, it should be noted that
at that time the supervisor was also mulling over whether *her*
bypass technique to circumvent ordinary supervisory obstacles
paralleled the patient's "back door" metaphor to circumvent
oedipal obstacles. The patient had been talking about working
during the coming year in a city far enough away to preclude
his continuing treatment with Dr. Jenkins, for pragmatic reasons
having to do with somewhat reduced finances and the common-
place occurrence in his field of frequent geographical relocations.
Dr. Jenkins learned of this *"suddenly,"* although her supervisor
had sensed it coming ever since the supervisee casually remarked
that her patient had begun to discuss these peripatetic aspects
of his work situation. At that time Dr. Jenkins was asked when
she intended to confront her patient with the obvious incom-
patibility between continuing analytic therapy with her and
pursuing his career elsewhere, as well as his wishfully based belief
that such a course of action would at last make possible a love
affair between himself and his therapist.

It became evident that Dr. Jenkins never made or even considered making such a confrontation. In fact, the patient strove
to maintain his illusion of a romance throughout the treatment
and never benefited from any proper therapeutic attempts to
analyze that fantasy and illusion within the transference. In a
highly significant related parallelism, Dr. Jenkins was concerned,
at least unconsciously, that she might have seduced the supervisor into believing she could do analysis eventually and have a
collegial peer relationship with her. It is also noteworthy that
she, like her patient, had then decided to terminate supervision
for "pragmatic" reasons: her work evaluations were open to
question; she was moving to a geographically less accessible area;
and she had embarked upon certain costly life changes, all of
which curtailed her pursuit of psychotherapy training. In this

instance, the supervisor identified that parallelism directly and explicitly labeled it as a parallelism. She pointed out that it seemed of great significance that she, the supervisee, in a manner paralleling her patient's vagueness about terminating treatment, had drifted into a course of action involving likely termination of formal training, supervision, and her personal analysis, and for pragmatic reasons, just as her patient did, and at an inopportune time. She surely could benefit from much more explicit discussion in supervision and other spheres of her training before deciding whether or not she could call herself an analytic therapist (she was planning to practice privately).

It was indeed unfortunate that Dr. Jenkins's own motivations and possible wishes to repudiate them had apparently interfered with the way she conducted the therapy, and they prevented her from dealing with her patient's critical negative transference resistance. The supervisor's approach conveyed to her that she was not seduced by *her* "psychological lie" that she was doing analytic therapy, but it was not clear to what extent she registered and assimilated what had been conveyed. It also is not clear if there would have been a different outcome had the supervisor handled the initial parallelism—her describing her patient as an as-if personality caught in a psychological lie—directly and not via the bypass operation. Had the supervisor talked of the parallelism of the patient's "A" for ambitious but imposturous success in his field and Dr. Jenkins's fantasied "A" for analytic therapy, she might have been decidedly correct as to a dynamic interpretation but incorrect with respect to supervisory dosage, timing, and tact.

Imposture, like the teaching and learning of psychoanalysis and psychoanalytic psychotherapy, indeed poses difficult problems for therapist or analyst and supervisor alike, particularly in the light of the real power that the supervisor has in being able to influence the future course of the supervisee's life as an analyst or analytic psychotherapist.

Part II

IN ART AND LIFE

INTRODUCTION TO THE ARTS: IMPOSTURE AND DECEIT IN ART AND LIFE

Part II is devoted to clinical psychoanalytic studies of the life and works of a famous artist and of a character in a play. We present rich sources of data other than those gleaned from the psychoanalytic encounter that substantiate some of our ideas about deception. In the first instance, we examine already existing writings about the personal life and artistic productions of the noted artist Arshile Gorky, who was rather universally regarded as imposturous and a liar. In the second, we attempt to expand our understanding of deceit by studying David Henry Hwang's (1989) play, *M. Butterfly*, a fictionalized account of a true story of imposturous cross-dressing and spying. This work informs some of our concluding remarks about the success of deception of audiences who are gullible in one degree or another.

The arts contain all kinds of deception. In fact all works of art make use of illusion, a primary form of deception, albeit one without pejorative connotation. Some art forms actually embody some of the more serious forms of deception that are to be found in real life. Consider, for example, grand opera, which is replete with characters disguising themselves in costume and demeanor as they masquerade as other characters. The plots of so many of the grand operas hinge on the success or lack of success of these deceptions, which are almost always with respect to gender or to rank. Deception in opera, which some would consider what opera is all about, deserves at least a monograph in itself, so its broad scope cannot be included in this book. However, a brief summary[1] of some of the highlights of deception in opera presents illustrations of cross-dressing and gender deception that are elaborated in Chapter 7 and generalized to several important social and clinical issues discussed in our concluding chapter.

Deception through the disguise of cross-dressing from male to female is found in the plots of many operas. In Mozart's *Le Nozze di Figaro,* for example, the male page, Cherubino, is dressed as a woman in Act II by the Countess and Susanna as part of Figaro's plot to thwart the plan of the count and to play a joke on him. Humor, illusion, and deception are maximized when the part of Cherubino is sung by a woman playing a man who is sometimes disguised as a woman. In addition to the male–female deception, *Figaro* contains the disguise of dressing with respect to rank when, in the last act, the maid Susanna and the Countess exchange clothes in order to fool the count and, also in a more serious vein, to foster the return of marital love. One might argue here that deception in such cases as these has some positive value, as do some of the white lies discussed in the first chapter.

In Richard Strauss's *Der Rosenkavalier*, Octavian, in Act I, disguises himself as a maid upon the entrance of Baron Ochs in the Feldmarschallin's boudoir, where she and Octavian are having a tryst. Act III involves a complicated joke on the Baron—a supposed tryst at an inn between himself and "Mariendal," who is Octavian, once again in female disguise. As in *Figaro*, to add to the humorous complications of deception, Octavian's role is

---

1. We thank Cecil K. Conklin for calling our attention to some important trends in instances of deception within operatic plots, and for providing us with a basis for this summary.

also sung by a woman playing a man sometimes disguised as a woman.

Female-to-male deception is another common theme in cross-dressing in opera. In Beethoven's *Fidelio*, the noble-woman Leonore, in a disguise that conceals her rank and status, dresses up as a man, Fidelio, in order to save her husband, a political prisoner chained in a dungeon. In this falsified condition, she apprentices herself to the jailor, a deception that involves an act of love and courage. This act has led some aficionados to regard her arguably as opera's gutsiest heroine, and is one more example of positive values placed on deception. To complicate matters, this opera contains a subplot involving Marcellina, the jailor's daughter, and Jacquino, who loves her. Deceiving Jacquino, Marcellina falls in love with Fidelio, and of course is astounded when she discovers that he is not a he but is Leonore in disguise!

In the last act of Verdi's *Rigoletto*, Rigoletto, who has arranged for the Duke's murder, tells his daughter Gilda to dress as a boy and to ride to Verona. She fakes her identity as instructed, but deceives her father by not going to Verona. She goes instead to the inn in order to sacrifice herself to save the Duke whom she loves but who is deceiving her in a rendezvous with another woman. Incidentally, this opera also contains disguise by rank, in Act I when the Duke, in wooing Gilda, disguises himself as a humble student.

Verdi's *La Forza del Destino* contains a complicated plot revolving around the accidental killing of Leonore di Vargas's father by her lover, Don Alvaro, and the long search by her brother, Don Carlo di Vargas, for revenge upon both of them. After the killing, Leonore leaves Seville disguised as a man and finally makes her way to a convent where she takes refuge.

From these few examples, it would seem that, when the cross-dressing is from male to female, it is usually humorous and part of a joke. When the cross-dressing is from female to male, however, its purpose is to allow the woman to do something she could not do as a woman; for example, "man's work" or traveling alone.

A major occurrence in opera, as in life, is the multitude of deceptions, if not literal disguise, involving marital infidelity. In Leoncavallo's *Pagliacci*, Pagliacci is deceived by his wife Nedda with Silvio; in Mascagni's *Cavalleria Rusticana*, Alfio is deceived by his wife Lola with Turiddu. It seems more difficult to find examples of marital infidelity by men, unless those men happen to be gods, as in Handel's *Semele*, in which the plot involves a philandering Jupiter and his angry wife Juno who plots to destroy the mortal, Semele. Similarly, in Wagner's *Der Ring des Nibelungen*, Wotan, ruler of the Norse gods, is a philandering husband, much to the ire of his wife Fricka. An apparent exception is Pinkerton in Puccini's *Madame Butterfly*, who does deceive Butterfly. However, since he never considered his arrangement with the Japanese woman to be a legal marriage, his deception may not be considered a bona-fide example of male marital infidelity in opera.

Finally, we find examples in opera of the *appearance* of deception by marital infidelity, adding another layer of meaning to our topic. In Verdi's *Un Ballo in Maschera*, Renato *thinks* his wife Amelia has been unfaithful with Riccardo, the King, and in the same composer's *Otello*, Iago deceives Otello about Desdemona's true feelings and actions. Iago also deceives Otello into thinking that he, Iago, is loyal and true. The plot of Mozart's *Così fan Tutte* revolves around the disguise of Ferrando and Guglielmo as Albanian soldiers in order to trick their girlfriends, Dorabella and Fiordiligi, into infidelity as part of a bet to see if they would be faithful. Once again, the idea that all women are prone to be fickle, "*La Donna e Mobile*," and generally dishonest with men is taken for granted, an idea that the early psychoanalysts might have believed to be consistent with an inferior superego development among women and with their capacity to fake orgasm, ideas that we dispute.

In Shakespeare's time, male actors dressed as women, and many of the bard's female characters disguised themselves as males within the context of the plays themselves. The audience, who were in the know, played along through the willing suspension of disbelief. Recent films, for example, *The Crying Game* and *Victor Victoria*, have delighted those who are duped as they identify with the characters in the film. The film, *Priscilla, Queen of the Desert*, makes the cross-dresser a most sympathetic, even admired character. In *M. Butterfly*, we also find these devices of double-duping, of cross-dressing, lying, and spying. It is not often that we see in our clinical practices those who have successfully masqueraded a false gender, and we rarely, if ever, get to treat spies in order to learn the psychology of the spy. In the field of literature, we cite George Sand, a woman writing under a man's name, and Thomas Mann's (1936) *The Confessions of Felix Krull*, the confidence man; more recently, writers such as John Le Carré have captivated their audiences with such stories as *The Little Drummer Girl* (1983), a genre in which spies, particularly double agents or "moles," devote a lifetime to imposturous functioning.

The issue of deception is an unstated and understated underpinning of the visual arts. All through the centuries artists have oscillated between attempts at depicting and copying reality and attempts at creating something completely new and original. In painting, the development of illusionistic techniques that enable the viewer to perceive objects as three dimensional when they are painted on two-dimensional flat canvasses, from trompe d'oeil to photorealist techniques, exemplify these positive and acceptable uses of deception. These trends were opposed by certain contemporary artists, for example, the minimalists. Frank Stella, for one, purported that his paintings were about paint and flatness: "What you see is what you see," nothing else. And, as Tomkins (1988) noted, "One of the founding beliefs of modernism was that it had become unnecessary and demeaning for art any longer to represent the external world. Instead of painting an imitation of something else—a trick to fool the eye—the modernist yearned to paint something that was real in itself, something that belonged to the world of art" (p. 221).

For example, the contemporary artist Duane Hanson has been able to make use of sophisticated materials in his sculptural works, which are primarily of elderly people who continue to deceive the spectator with their illusion of reality. Those who know that these figures are actually sculptures continue to experience them as real people and continue to delight in having been deceived. Balter (1994) has recently attempted to explain the aesthetic illusion, or why people experience art as reality. He believes that the distinctive nature of aesthetic communication results in the illusion that the artistic daydream is really the beholder's own, and that the artist is irrelevant or nonexistent.

Artists learn, for the most part, through long periods of imitation, by copying the works of others. This imitation is considered to be quite appropriate, unless the copied work is passed off as original and sold as such. In this case the forgery itself is the deception. In recent years, postmodern thinking has deconstructed the formerly supreme value placed on originality. Art that can be mechanically reproduced is in vogue. Appropriating, "referencing," and "quoting" the works of other artists, as in rephotography, have become legitimate endeavors. The concept of the simalcrum, or copy of a copy, is perhaps an art history analogue of Riesenberg-Malcolm's (1990) "slicing," a form of resistance in which the analyst's interpretation is watered down by the patient so as to render it less vital than it was in its original form.

The concepts of the masquerade and the carnivalesque have also been part of art history, from Velasquez's court jesters, to Longhi's masked Venetians, to the work of the contemporary gay black artist Lyle Ashton Harris, who photographed himself in drag and in whiteface, a tulle ballerina's costume draped around his naked penis.

In Chapter 6, we examine the life and works of the artist Arshile Gorky (1904–1948), who emigrated from Armenia to America in 1920. We note changes in his imposturous tendencies over time. Gorky's works in the early part of his career were highly derivative and were produced at a time when he manifested personality disturbances of profound identity confusion, with tendencies to lie, to camouflage, and to be fraudulent. This pathology seemed to have resulted from a childhood "holocaust" experience in which he and his family were subjected to the Turkish genocidal attempt on the Armenians. At the outbreak of this attempt, his father abandoned his family; at the end, his mother died of starvation. The work of Pollock (1989) and others is used to support the thesis that the act of painting itself can be restorative and ameliorative. It is proposed that Gorky's ten years of work on *The Artist and His Mother* enabled him to complete an unfinished mourning process for his dead mother; and his copying of the works of great artists, all of whom were male, enabled him to further internalize a father figure. He was able then, to some degree and for some time, to free himself from the mantle of guilt-induced poverty and profound suffering he wore, to marry, to have children, and to function so as to win critical acclaim. He was able to work in a unique painting style characterized by lush sensuous color and surrealist biomorphic form, a style that bore the imprint of intensely powerful unconscious fantasy and affect. An unfortunate series of traumatic events, possibly experienced by him as a recapitulation of childhood traumata, resulted in profound regression and his ultimate suicide.

In Chapter 7, we consider the experience of viewing the play *M. Butterfly*, of being duped by a man masquerading as a woman, an experience shared by protagonist and audience alike. In a parallel process, both simultaneously know and do not know the realities of the impostor's gender. Cross-dressing, as a variety of imposture, is explained by expanding on Freud's (1927) contribution of the "fantasy of the phallic woman." A full psychoanalytic understanding of perverse and fetishistic resolutions of early developmental conflicts about the nature of gender requires a consideration of the fear of the vagina along with the wish for a woman with a phallus. This approach to a study of imposture suggests that fantasies shared in common by all people help account for the success of even gross impostures.

THE IMPOSTUROUS ARTIST ARSHILE GORKY: FROM IDENTITY CONFUSION TO IDENTITY SYNTHESIS

INTRODUCTION

Arshile Gorky is considered to be one of America's foremost artists. The ideas of Gorky, a proto-abstract expressionist, were seminal influences on the works of Willem de Kooning, Mark Rothko, Jackson Pollock, and others. As a young man, he worked in a rather stilted, intellectualized painting style that was derived from European cubism. He was then greatly influenced by surrealism and developed a unique fluid style characterized by its use of biomorphic forms and lyrical color freed from line. Using a technique called automatism, in which the artist allows whatever images emerge mentally to be translated onto the canvas via his hand and the brush, Gorky was able to reach into his unconscious in a process similar to that of the analysand who says whatever comes to mind. In lieu of words, the visual images

Note: This chapter is based on a paper presented by Janice S. Lieberman, Ph.D., "Arshile Gorky: From Identity Diffusion to Identity Synthesis," at the New York Freudian Society, January 1991, and at Division 39 of the American Psychological Association, Chicago, April 1991.

retrieved were then placed on the canvas in an order and arrangement of his own creation.

The vicissitudes of Gorky's life, as well as of his works, are of particular interest to one who is psychoanalytically trained. Gorky was not analyzed, and therefore, the nature of the comments made about him in this chapter are *entirely speculative*, as they are in most psychobiographies. His many biographers from the worlds of art, art history, and art criticism have made psychologically informed comments about him and his tendencies to imposturousness, notably Harold Rosenberg (1962, 1964), Ethel Schwabacher (1957), Diane Waldman (1981), Melvin Lader (1985), and his nephew Karlan Mooradian (1955, 1967, 1971, 1978). The psychoanalyst-critic Donald Kuspit (1987) has also written a Kohutian commentary entitled "Arshile Gorky: Images in Support of the Invented Self," that is referred to in the forthcoming discussion.

Gorky, who was born in Armenia in 1904, was beset by a series of devastating, traumatic events that began during his childhood: paternal abandonment, starvation, and exile during the Turkish genocidal attempt on the Armenians; his mother's death from starvation; and emigration to the United States at the age of 16. Nevertheless, he was able to be productive both as an artist and as a teacher throughout his life. His many friends regarded him as lovable, but with imposturous tendencies they could not begin to address. He told stories about himself that were inconsistent, with constant shifts in name, date, place, and action. His appearance was profoundly melancholy, and he always seemed to be much older than he actually was. At the age of 44 he suffered a mental breakdown and hanged himself after a series of incredible events that were most likely experienced internally as a recapitulation of his childhood holocaust-like experiences. We regard his story as a case study of imposturousness and confirmatory of hypotheses presented earlier in this book about the antecedent personal history and psychic structure typical of imposturousness.

In this chapter parallels are noted between certain changes in Gorky's personal identity, as it developed and became more cohesive in the consistent and stable American environment, and concurrent transformations in his painting style. That style evolved from a derivative and somewhat rigid one to one with an original, fluid, and imaginative form. We show how Gorky's use of several "Great Artists" as idealized father figures, along with his decade of work on a series of self-portraits, in particular two versions of *The Artist and His Mother* (ca. 1929–1942 [see Figure 6–1], 1926–1929), possibly facilitated a restorative process of internalization and a working through of mourning for his dead mother. One can assume that a "mourning–liberation process" (Pollock 1989) was operative.

The series of traumatic childhood events seem to have produced in the young Gorky a profound state of identity confusion. He slavishly copied the style of other artists—not just ordinary artists, but the greats, Uccello, Ingres, and especially Cezanne, Picasso, and Miro—long past the time during which imitation is useful for an artist. An example is *Painting* (1936–1937, see Figure 6–2). His choice of whom to imitate was quite personal; for example, he was said to have chosen to emulate Picasso rather than Braque because he shared a sense of estrangement with Picasso. For a time, his works were indistinguishable from those of his friend John Graham. His identity confusion manifested itself (1) in the prolonged period of copying already described; (2) in his proclivity to lying and deception; (3) in manifestations of a fraudulence bordering upon imposturousness; (4) in an opaque, covered-over quality in his personality that was likened to camouflage; (5) in his idiosyncratic use of the English language, beyond the bounds one might expect in one who adopts a new language in adulthood; and (6) in a profound melancholy and seriousness that expressed his unfinished mourning of the loss of his father, his mother, his homeland, and his childhood grandiosity, a process fueled by what the psychoanalyst would reconstruct as the tremendous burden of unconscious guilt.

Art scholars have speculated that Gorky's copying of great male artists, abnegating his own personality in the process,

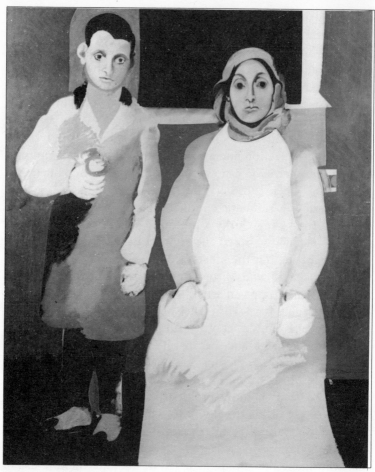

Figure 6–1. Arshile Gorky: *The Artist and His Mother*. Collection of Whitney Museum of American Art, New York. Gift of Julien Levy for Maro and Natasha Gorky in memory of their father. Photo: Geoffrey Clements, Staten Island, NY.

Figure 6–2. Arshile Gorky: *Painting*. Collection of Whitney Museum of American Art, New York. Photo: Geoffrey Clements, Staten Island, NY.

enabled him to reach a higher level of psychological integration. By identifying with these idealized figures, by slowly internalizing them, he was able to work through and restore the narcissistic loss of his father, who abandoned his family in an act of cowardice, and who was most likely demeaned in the eyes of his more educated, aristocratic mother. In Gorky's "surrender" to these great artists, he would make statements that indicated the adhesiveness of his identifications. For example, in speaking of Picasso, he said: "If he drips, I drip" (quoted in Rosenberg 1962, p. 66). His identifications were more than identifications, verging on, but not precisely the same as imposture and plagiarism, for he not only copied Picasso's styles but also his various signatures and placement of signatures on the canvas. He said, "I feel Picasso running in my fingertips" (quoted in Reiff 1977, p. 215).

The inner reparation and restoration that we assume took place as a result of his working on *The Artist and his Mother* enabled Gorky in his late thirties to marry, to have children and a fine home, and to give up the mantle of suffering and poverty that he had worn all his life. He was then able to develop a unique painting style as exemplified by *The Betrothal II*, (1947, see Figure 6–3) and no longer needed to draw from others in order to create.

CHRONOLOGY OF GORKY'S LIFE (1904–1948)

As mentioned, several biographies of Gorky's life and voluminous files of his letters and writings are available for scrutiny. Nevertheless, some basic facts, such as dates and places, appear in different form from biography to biography, creating in the researcher a sense of shaky incertitude—akin to an induced countertransference—as to exactly who this person was and exactly what took place in his life. The brief history we have pieced together from these sources is elaborated upon in the next section of this chapter.

Figure 6–3. Arshile Gorky: *The Betrothal*. Collection of Whitney Museum of American Art, New York. Photo: Geoffrey Clements, Staten Island, NY.

Gorky was born in 1904 in the village of Khorkom, in eastern Armenia. His real name was Vosdanik Manook Adoian. His father, of peasant background, was a trader and carpenter who supported Gorky's aunts and uncles, all of whom lived together under one roof. His mother, highly educated and beautiful, came from a line of exalted priests. Both parents were quite tall, supposedly the only trait they really had in common. Gorky himself grew to be 6'4" as an adult. He had two sisters, three and eight years older, and one sister two years younger. As a young child, his mother helped foster his artistic vision by taking him to visit various cathedrals and shrines, where he saw (and never forgot) illuminated manuscripts with their calligraphy and exotic hybrid human and animal forms. From the age of 4, he obsessively and constantly carved and sculpted wood.

At that crucial age of 4, Gorky's father left abruptly for America in order to avoid the Turkish draft. At the age of 8, now man of the house, he posed for the photograph with his mother—his sisters were not included—that served as the basis for *The Artist and His Mother*. This photograph was to be sent to his father, who was by then living in Rhode Island. In 1914 to 1915, when he was 10, the Turks seized his city and began the extermination of the Armenians. The family's house was shelled, and he, his mother, and his sisters went on a death march to the Caucasus. They lost everything. They had buried their possessions in the ground, but were never to return. The churches and manuscripts he had grown to love were also destroyed. Mother and children moved from place to place. His mother and sisters took in some sewing despite the fact that in their culture women who worked disgraced the men in the family. Gorky as man of the family had to work for the little they were to have. His two older sisters then left for America, and at the age of 15, he was to hold his mother in his arms as she died of starvation while dictating a last letter to his father in Rhode Island. He and his younger sister, dressed in rags, were helped by family friends to travel to Constantinople, then Greece, and then to the United States. After a brief stay with his father in Rhode Island, and after retrieving the photograph, he went to live in Watertown, Massachusetts, with his oldest sister and her family. He went to work in a factory, but lost his job because he spent his time drawing rather than working. At the age of 16, he took the name Gorky, a Greek word for "the bitter one." Arshile is an equivalent of Achilles. He remained in close contact with his sisters and their families throughout his life, but it is unclear how much contact he ever maintained with his father.

After studying art in Boston, he came to New York in 1925, set up a studio in Greenwich Village, and at 21 years of age taught art and published important-sounding pronouncements about his philosophy of art. For the next ten to twelve years his works were for the most part imitations of and derivations of the works of the greats. In 1930, he moved his studio to Union Square, where he befriended Willem de Kooning, John Graham, and Stuart Davis, among other artists, with whom he interacted intensively. They debated and learned from one another about art making. His studio was noted for its immaculateness, its orderliness, and its huge stockpile of artists' supplies that put him into debt and often led to his suffering from starvation. During this period of the Depression, Gorky was noted for his impoverished look. His clothes always had holes in them. He subsisted on doughnuts and coffee during a time when the WPA paid him $37 a week to do murals at Newark Airport. Constantly critical of American values, he chose as lovers American women whom he sought to remake into deeper, more intellectual persons. In 1935 he was married briefly to a Midwestern woman, Marney George, a student of fashion art. The marriage ended when she resisted his attempts to reform her in accordance with his preferences and ideals. According to his nephew Mooradian, being an Armenian was problematic for him, and he felt blocked in praising his homeland, now under the Soviet regime.

From 1936 to 1937, he did an abstract composition called *Painting*, which was purchased by the Whitney Museum of American Art. At about that time, he completed, or shall we say let go of, *The Artist and His Mother*, which he had begun in 1926.

Life took a different turn for Gorky. He met and married Agnes Magruder, a straight, fearless, and quite beautiful young Bostonian. Perhaps he had found in her his mother imago, or more likely, he was free enough of his conflictual attachment to his mother, having mourned her death sufficiently to allow himself to love and be loved once again. Agnes seemed to give this incredibly unhappy man a center. He asked her to cook his mother's favorite recipes. Their domestic bliss resulted in their having two daughters, Maro, born in 1943, and Natasha, born in 1945. They lived in several attractive houses and finally purchased an architecturally remarkable glass house in Sherman, Connecticut.

During this period (1942–1948), his unique surrealistic style flourished. A series of one-man shows at the Julien Levy Gallery began to receive critical acclaim. However, at the height of his success, a series of tragedies occurred. A fire broke out in the chimney of his studio in 1945, destroying that year's work. He suspected his wife of having an affair with his colleague and protegé, Matta. He developed cancer and had a colostomy. In 1948 he was hurt in a car accident, breaking his neck and causing his painting arm to be temporarily paralyzed. Dark mood swings and suspiciousness ensued, alienating his wife, who, with their children, left him to go to her parents' house. Two weeks later, at the age of 44, he hanged himself.

THE FORMATIVE YEARS: PSYCHIC TRAUMA

The series of traumas that accumulated in the life of young Gorky are now described in more detail. These accounts are distillations of stories Gorky personally told friends and biographers, with all the possibilities for distortion and elaboration that exist in such tellings and that we are familiar with in the material provided us by our analysands. At the age of 4, he, his mother, and his sisters were profoundly abandoned by his father. His father put the children on a horse, told them to ride out into the field, eat lunch, and then return to their mother. He presented young Gorky with the pair of red slippers that were to be a repeated motif in his works. The children returned to find their father gone. This experience supposedly left Gorky speechless, and he refused to speak until a year later when, as he later told it, his tutor threatened to jump from a cliff unless he spoke. Coincidentally, the artist Louise Nevelson (1976), in writing of her early childhood in Russia, reported that "I was about three when my father went to America, and my mother told me that for one half year, I didn't speak. And they thought I had become deaf and dumb" (p. 6).

From that point on, a precocious maturity, as symbolized by the gift of the slippers (to "walk in his father's shoes"), was imposed upon the young Gorky, perhaps by himself, perhaps by his family, but most probably, by a combination of both. He was the responsible and only male in the family, treasured above his sisters because he was male. He was breadwinner, oedipal winner, and sibling winner. One might speculate that he experienced much unconscious resentment at his father's leaving him, depriving him of his support as a role model and as a protector against internal anxieties. One might also speculate that he developed unconscious guilt over these feelings, having been made so explicitly his mother's favorite, and that a regression to anal levels of obsessiveness and ambivalent object relations ensued. His biographer, Ethel Schwabacher (1957), provides us with a confirmatory memory, which might well be a screen memory that partially masks an earlier event. As in much of the biographical material about Gorky, one reporter's story tends to shift slightly from another's with respect to the age at which given events supposedly occurred. Schwabacher quotes Gorky:

> I remember myself when I was 5 years old. The year I first began to speak. Mother and I are going to church. We are there. For a while she left me standing before a painting. It was a painting of infernal regions. There were angels in the painting. White angels and black angels. All the black angels were going to Hades. I

looked at myself. I am black too. It means there is no Heaven for me. A child's heart could not accept it. And I decided there and then to prove to the world that a black angel can be good too, must be good and wants to give his inner goodness to the whole world, black and white world. [p. 104]

In *The Family Romance of the Artist*, Greenacre (1971) writes:

> Family romance fantasies of a well-organized nature seem to emerge most clearly in the early latency period; are indicative of a marked degree of ambivalence to the parents, especially due to grossly unresolved Oedipal problems. This ambivalence seems reinforced by the ambivalence of the anal period to which good and bad, applied to the self and to the parent, appear like black and white twins in so many relationships. [p. 507]

From Gorky's words, it may be hypothesized that the low self-esteem and the splitting mechanisms of the imposturous adult, of which Greenacre speaks, were already in place.

During latency and early adolescence, Gorky went to school as much as was feasible, but had to work to supply his family with food. We speculate once more about the emergence of feelings of guilt and a profound sense of inadequacy when his mother died in his arms, as well as a feeling of betrayal, for his mother died while writing to his father. He was disqualified in his prior attempts to place her in a hospital for homeless genocide victims because his father was still alive and believed to be capable of sending them money, which in fact he never did.

Gorky's experience of the Turkish genocide of the Armenian people was a holocaust experience. At the age of 10, he witnessed murder, rape, starvation, pillage, thousands turning black as they died of cholera, and mounds of bodies that had to be buried in order to prevent disease from spreading. He and his family were homeless, wandering. Barefoot and in rags, Gorky and his younger sister left for America. All ties with homeland, with place and folk, were amputated. From feudal Asia Minor, they were transplanted to a Western industrial society.

THE ADAPTIVE EGO

How does a child survive such unspeakable traumata? Massive defenses such as splitting and dissociation are generally erected against internal pain. Certain fantasies of specialness serve a restitutive function when one is abandoned, rejected, persecuted, rendered helpless. Gorky's heritage on his mother's side was a proud one. As has been said, she was of a long line of exalted priests. He described her as follows (quoted in Mooradian 1978): "She was the most aesthetically appreciative, the most poetically incisive master I have encountered in all my life. Mother was queen of the aesthetic domain" (p. 104). She encouraged his artistic talent and an awareness of his Armenian heritage by taking him to see the beautiful shrines and cathedrals with their extended iconography of hybrid men and animals. She made certain he had art supplies. We speculate that in his art making, he was able to hold on to this strong mother during difficult times as if in a curative cocoon, removed from fear or pain. Gorky was, in a way, tunnel-blind to all else. Art seemed to function as his libidinal object throughout his life. A year before his death he wrote in a letter (dated January 1, 1947): "Art must always remain earnest . . . must be serious, no sarcasm, comedy. One does not laugh at a loved one" (Mooradian 1978, p. 42). Eisenstadt and colleagues (1989), in their study of parental loss and achievement, write that an overidealization of a dead parent results in an attempt to achieve, to restore. The creative product will "on the one hand, alleviate those feelings of guilt and, on the other hand, prove to all the world the individual's essential goodness" (p. 26). In their study, subtitled *Orphans and the Will for Power*, they found that a disproportionate number of those who lose parents during childhood became creative geniuses, the political leaders of the past centuries. They view parent loss as a stimulant that can "lead to the creativity necessary to resolve the issues of formation, identity, and feelings of emptiness" (frontispiece). Creativity, of course, is only one outcome of such trauma. There may be bleaker ones for the nongifted.

Further confirmation of the theory that Gorky's art was tied up with his attachment to and identification with his mother is evident in a letter written in 1935: "Just as a woman bears children and again becomes pregnant, so I again become pregnant with new ideas and remain determined to perfect my work" (Mooradian 1971, p. 54). In a letter of January 6, 1947, the year before he died, he wrote to his sister and her children: "Art is such a delicious food. It is nutrition and medicine wrapped in a soft bundle" (Mooradian 1978, p. 300).

Gorky, as the only male in his family, was singled out as special. His sisters later told tales of his phallic exploits, riding an Arabian horse in the mountains. The Armenian culture held a paradoxical view of women. Women were on the one hand venerated, and they even fought in revolutionary movements. But they were also demeaned. For example, they ate separately from men. A bride entering a new household initiated conversation with her husband's family only a year after the birth of a child. Gorky as a male child was so valuable that, when there was a scarcity of food, any food his mother found was given to him rather than to his sisters; she took nothing for herself.

Those who have had such a chain of experiences usually find a rationalizing philosophy to hang onto. Gorky is quoted (Mooradian 1978), as follows: "My life resembles our wavy sea: exploding with turbulence and tempered by sorrow, but that is not necessarily a bad thing, for storms attain certain aesthetic purity only after cleansing themselves by charging over many rocks and barriers before reaching the beauty of the soft shore" (p. 252).

Donald Kuspit's (1987) Kohutian analysis of Gorky emphasizes the injury to his sense of self-worth: "The trauma of being uprooted, and having to put down new roots undermined Gorky's sense of self, narcissistically injured him, and necessitated fresh self-creation. Gorky had to become a new person or he would be nobody. And he could only become a new self by

planting his old self in the new soil of the American landscape"
(p. 203).

THE ADULT PSYCHE

Although he survived, Gorky paid an enormous psychic price
for this survival. He arrived in the United States at the age of 16
with a remarkable talent and a capacity to live and to work
independently. However, he was to be for perhaps the next
twenty or so years in a state of profound identity confusion. He
had not sufficiently internalized a male role model, he had not
yet, as far as we know, been able to mourn his mother's death,
and he did not accept his being transplanted from one world to
the other.

Harold Rosenberg (1962), the critic and his biographer,
wrote of Gorky's copying of the works of the great artists: "His
own work is almost a visual metaphor of the digestion of European painting on this side of the Atlantic and its conversion
into a new substance" (p. 1). Gorky's rationalization was that
only after an artist had "digested" the great art of the past could
he hope to rival it. It was as if he lived with each artist, one at
a time, in order to absorb him and incorporate him. His self-
portraits were shaky, problematic, and not truly reflective of
who he was, an indicator of that unstable sense of self we have
come to recognize as a hallmark of unstable identifications. In
1964, Rosenberg wrote: "None of the Gorky portraits is a good
likeness and in this respect his self-portraits are least good.
Gorky could not grasp himself even as appearance" (p. 102).
Gorky would say: "I was *with* Cezanne for a long time and now
naturally I am *with* Picasso" (quoted in Waldman 1981, p. 24).
Rosenberg commented, "Until his last year, no new idea ever
shows itself in Gorky all of a piece; it pokes, then recedes into
the canon he is following. There is no end to his apprentice-
ship; yet at every stage, he reaches ahead to things of his own"
(1962, p. 48).

More problematic than characterological identity problems of imposture was Gorky's tendency toward outright lying and deception, toward what Rosenberg (1962) termed "a higher mathematics of pseudonymity which was to be characteristic of his art" (p. 42). That is, in some respects he was a true impostor, one who misrepresents himself by assuming an identity or title not his own. He took the name Arshile Gorky and passed himself off as a Russian, the cousin of a nephew of the great writer Maxim Gorky (whose name was also a pseudonym). The Armenian villager thus became a cultivated Russian. One can speculate that Gorky, like so many artists, was motivated by underlying family romance fantasies. Greenacre (1958b) cites such cases, in which the real parents, replaced in fantasy by noble and exalted ones, were decathected and punished for their sexuality. As Diane Waldman (1981), in her catalogue for the Guggenheim Museum, reflected:

> Gorky was no stranger to romantic legend, forever telling exotic and conflicting stories about his origins, posing variously as Russian, Georgian, Armenian; speaking of himself as a relative of Maxim Gorky and as a pupil of Kandinsky, a student of the Polytechnic Institute in Tiflis, a student at the Academie Julien in Paris or at Brown University, when in fact he was far too young to have undertaken such advanced studies. [p. 16]

Some of these lies were never corrected by Gorky or others. For example, after his death, an article in the *New York Times* still reported him as a cousin of Maxim Gorky and a Russian. When his younger daughter was born, she was listed as Yalda. Then her Armenian name was changed to the Russian Natasha, possibly related to some repetition of his own name change. The artist Elaine de Kooning (1951) wrote of Gorky:

> He would fabricate or embellish incidents of his personal history, shuffle a few dates in his paintings, sign his name to a couple of essays he never wrote, and pass off as his own lines from the few poems he had read. A biography was something to hide behind.

He told people he was born in three different countries in three different years. He told friends he did not speak until he was 6— before that only with birds. [p. 39]

His love letters to various women contained the poems of Paul Eluard, which he presented as his own.

In our attempt to understand Gorky's plagiarisms and other kinds of fraudulence as a form of imposturousness, we speculate that Gorky's superego was formed on the basis of an absent paternal introject. His own father, in a way, lied to him by not telling him of his planned departure. His father was not there in reality to inhibit (or to castrate) and could not serve to curb his son's arrogance. It does not seem like too big a leap to interpret that Gorky's search for the lost father and wishes to resurrect him within himself appear as an important dynamic in his various imitations and wishful identity fabrications.

Erikson (1968), quoted in Chapter 4 on the imposture and inauthenticity of an American girl of Middle European origins who created for herself an identity as Scottish, observes that, in some cases of identity confusion, estrangement from national and ethnic origins leads to a complete denial of the true roots of personal identity, and confabulatory reconstructions of one's origins are invented. This reinvented, fantasized account of the parents as glorified covers over a death wish toward the parents who are in fact devalued (pp. 173–174). If Erikson's conclusions are applicable to Gorky's case, the artist's imposturous tendencies might account for the fate of his aggressive drive, for strong aggression and even impotent rage seem to have been stimulated by the helplessness he experienced in the face of his father's abandonment, his mother's death, and the precocious maturity that was imposed on him and that he chose to develop in an attempt to master the traumatic sense of helplessness. Another way to understand Gorky's denial of his own true identity is afforded us by Loewald's (1979) notion, which we introduced in Chapter 4 in our discussion of the unconscious meanings of authenticity and autonomy. That is, to develop an authentic sense of identity and an experience of oneself as agent can be equated unconsciously with replacing the oedipal parent as though by committing parricide. Erikson (1968) refers to imposture as a severe identity crisis in which, via the "negative identity" of imposture, there is a hateful repudiation of the most dangerous and yet the most real identifications with the parents at various critical stages of development over the life cycle.

The critic, Harold Rosenberg (1962), considered Gorky to be a paradoxical figure and was quite suspicious of him. This amateur psychologist astutely pointed to certain inconsistencies, which psychoanalysts understand as reflecting unintegrated parts of the ego, when he wrote, "The immigrant is a self-made man; making oneself (self-creation) is not, however, far distant from making oneself up (self-disguise). When, in arriving in America, Gorky decided to become an artist, he decided at the same time to *look* like an artist" (1962, pp. 22–23). Rosenberg (1962) described Gorky's "pleading, war-orphan" eyes and went on to write "that this Bohemian type, always ready to put on the neglected genius act, especially in the presence of women and important people, should be at the same time a relentless thinker and disciplined creator in a puzzle designed to baffle moralizers and mislead swindlers" (p. 24).

Psychoanalysts, however, can grasp the paradoxical closeness between feelings of authenticity as opposed to inauthenticity among the creative, a closeness that challenges some common moralizing stereotypes about truth and falsehood, honesty and deception. In general, one can discern an important connection between creation among the truly creative, such as Gorky, and the self-creation of imposturous individuals, such as Gorky. One might also speculate that Gorky never felt sure of himself, that is, was not in touch with his true self, because of significant lacunae not just in superego but in true self development, and, paradoxically, he had to cultivate his false self through his adoptive identities in order to feel authentic.

Lying helps maintain repression of painful memories. As we noted earlier in Chapter 3 on lying, Fenichel (1939) describes how lying and deception could disguise unconscious fantasies and wishes; that is, they are defensively motivated. He states the rationale of the liar: "If I can make others believe the things which I know to be untrue are true, then it is also possible that my memory is deceived and what I remember as true is untrue" (p. 136). Gorky's "cover" perhaps enabled him to hold back the tide of painful childhood experiences so that he could go on with his life and his work.

Abraham (1925), Deutsch (1955), Gediman (1985), and Greenacre (1958a) describe characters who are somewhat like, but also different from, Gorky. The true impostor, as we noted, pretends under someone else's name, whereas those who are imposturous to a lesser degree—for example, as-if personalities—pretend, with great interest in imitation, under someone else's style and role, taking on the color of those who are admired and idealized. Although the true impostor suffers from serious arrests and deficits in ego development, those with lesser imposturous tendencies often behave in ways generally considered to be neurotic, such as from a need for punishment.

Continuing his self psychological analysis, Kuspit (1987) concludes: "Gorky, moving from mentor to mentor, searching for a new identity as soon as the old one became an 'act,' was perpetually destroying himself and being reborn as someone else until finally he was reborn as himself" (p. 205).

Gorky was reported to have been highly defended: "to Gorky at that time, nothing was more fenced off than his real self" (Rosenberg 1964, p. 100). His dealer, Julien Levy, called him a "camouflaged man," and it is of interest to note that in the early part of World War II he volunteered to teach a course on camouflage. This psychological covering over might have been an influence on his tendency to overpaint. His canvases were extremely heavy due to his painting layer on layer of image, a characteristic that art historians attribute to the scarcity of materials. Gorky's very appearance was experienced by many as staged rather than authentic. Word had gotten out that even his moustache and beard were his inventions to mask the real world from which he came and to create a new world in which he wished to belong. As has been said, Rosenberg described him as playing the role of the "Great Artist," according to Bohemian stereotype. Stuart Davis (1957) did not even believe that Gorky was poor, for he was the only artist who in those days had a studio. The critic Barbara Rose (1986) reported that Gorky's demeanor and intense gaze impelled one woman to ask if he were Jesus Christ, to which he replied: "Madame, I am Arshile Gorky" (p. 73).

Even in his mourning and nostalgia for his homeland, Gorky did not receive much sympathy from his friends. He induced contempt and scorn rather than sympathy in others, especially men. We wonder if he was unconsciously seeking punishment in a masochistic way. Rosenberg (1962) described his showman's use of his past as an Armenian peasant. He would sing folk songs and do shepherds' dances. His close friends eventually forbade these demonstrations in their presence. From photographs and from his letters and writings it was apparent that he was quite sad, seemed older than his age, and was never vibrant or smiling. His immaculate shiny, colorful studio in the 1930s contrasted greatly with the dark despair and the soul-crushing isolation he experienced inside himself during those years. He forever mourned his homeland, never adapting to commercial America, feeling that although it was rich in technology, it was poor in humanism. He wrote on August 1, 1939 (Mooradian 1971), "I always feel alone, even when I see my many friends and am among the thousands" (p. 104).

The child who once refused to speak grew up to be a compulsive talker as an adult, one of his many apparently compulsive defenses, like his arrogance and his imposture. He spoke almost exclusively about art and his philosophy of art. He spoke while painting, while giving interviews, and while taking people to museums and galleries. His speech was strange—his letters are poetically eloquent, but difficult to understand. One might attribute this strangeness to a different thought pattern, to the translation from Armenian to English, but it seems to be something more than that. Stuart Davis (1951) described it this way: "It was no mere matter of a foreign accent, though that was present, but an earthquake-like effect on sentence structure and a savagely perverse use of words to mean something they didn't" (p. 57). This typically imposturous use of words was not just an affectation, but like so much else in Gorky's defensive armamentarium, can be understood as a narcissistically compensatory attempt. It helped him cover over a feeling of inauthenticity, perhaps related to his early entitlement fantasies, or was based on his being an oedipal winner who perhaps committed, in his imagination, a successful but premature parricide.

As Gorky became more integrated, he invented a visual language, that is, he went from verbal to visual expression of what was inside himself. As his private, internal images were placed on the canvas, he adopted the surrealist's use of enigmatic titles that were highly personal and/or titles of poems and other literary works.

THE ARTIST AND HIS MOTHER
(CA. 1929–1942 AND 1926–1929)
AND ITS INFLUENCE ON HIS LATER WORKS

In these two transitional paintings, the first of which is illustrated in Figure 6–1, Gorky worked in a style that was quite different from the early cubist or late surrealist styles he is noted for. There are echoes of Ingres and Picasso in these portraits, polished as if they were jewels and breathtaking to behold. They show how adept he was at unifying two-dimensional and three-dimensional forms in a powerful totality. The portrait is drawn from memory and from the famous photo he took with his mother at age 8, a photo intended for his father to see. The pose is therefore not psychologically dyadic but triadic. His three sisters are excluded. He is carefully dressed. His mother, the Lady Shushenik of the priestly Armenian family, radiates with nobility and self-sacrifice. In the painting he creates a sense of intimacy absent in the photo.

Karp (1982) points out that the painting calls to mind Dietrich's (1990) "lost immortal parent complex," in which the object is both lost and immortal, frozen in space, yet not spatially bound, a beloved parent that the individual seeks or hopes will return.

Viederman (1990), in his study of Edvard Munch, examines a recurrent shape in Munch's paintings that seems to derive from a photo of the artist on his mother's lap. He reconstructs this motif as Munch's attempt to put together a coherent picture of his mother's death and to communicate this event to others. The work done is in the service of adaptation and integration. The use of the photo, in Gorky's case, can also be understood as serving a function akin to that of a transitional object.

Rosenberg (1964) calls *The Artist and his Mother* a "missing link" between the early imitative drawings and the canvases of the last phase (1942–1948): "in double portrait, Gorky reached for identity in the direction of his actual self and away from the Great Artist 'role-playing'" (p. 105). His venture into surrealism eased his communication with his childhood and loosened his concept of art and the artist so that he became closer to himself and no longer had to relate to the Great Works or resort to imposture. Waldman (1981) wrote that Gorky for the first time was able to connect with his own past and personal identity.

According to Sandler (1970), Gorky's independence was facilitated by his relationship with Andre Breton, who became another father figure to him but was not a fantasy father since they had a real relationship. The surrealists gave him the confidence he needed to rely on his own intuition, insight, and expressiveness. We hypothesize that the period of dependency and the protracted labor on *The Artist and His Mother* both integrated him to a greater degree and enabled him to use himself as a creative source.

Pollock (1989), in his study of the artist Käthe Kollwitz, writes that in certain individuals "great creativity may not be the successful outcome of the successfully completed mourning process but may be indicative of attempts at completing the mourning work. These creative attempts may be conceptualized as restitution, reparation, discharge, or sublimation" (p. 571).

Rosenberg (1962) wrote of the new style that then emerged: "Literally beside himself, that is, acting outside the limits of his self-consciousness, Gorky can now make manifest in his paintings and drawings psychological states he had formerly confided only in private relations. Eroticism flooded his soul of a Puritan" (p. 103). Opulent sexual imagery was especially evident in his *Garden in Sochi* series of 1940–1943 about which Gorky wrote: "The garden was identified as the Garden of Wish Fulfillment and often I had seen my mother and other village women opening their bosoms and taking their soft and dependable breasts in their hands to wash them on the rocks" (quoted in Rose 1986, p. 73).

Donald Kuspit (1987) saw the works of this period as a restoration of the self-object, of the primal father–son relationship, an attempt "to recapture, through Modernist means, the primitive spirit of 'authentic' [his own word] nature, with its miraculously generative tree symbolic of the imagination as such—he is more completely dependent than ever on self-objects. He has found his way back to his true father, to the supreme self-object" (pp. 201–202). Kuspit's thesis is that Gorky imagined he had done something bad by being banished from his father's garden and tried to heal this through his art.

When, in 1941, Gorky met and married Agnes Magruder, and their two daughters were born, he was finally to experience joy in his life. His domestic bliss might have been experienced by him as a reliving of the time he lived happily with his family in Armenia before he was 4 years old. He gave up his asceticism and allowed himself to have a telephone and good meals, to work outdoors, and to reacquaint himself with the joys of nature.

At this time the series of tragic events described earlier occurred. In February of 1945, his studio, with all the work he had done that year, was destroyed by fire. This fire might have revived, whether consciously or unconsciously, the memory of something he knew as a child. Gorky believed that he had been born with a curse, for his maternal grandmother, one year before his birth, warred against the God of the Armenians by setting fire to the family's ancestral church upon finding his young uncle's body lying in front of the church door with a Turkish dagger in his back (Mooradian 1967). He was then diagnosed as having cancer of the colon and had a colostomy in February, 1946. These events left him psychologically although not physically impotent. The colostomy bag he had to wear was unpalatable to the fastidious Gorky. His work went well, but shades of paranoia were becoming manifest, as is evident in a letter to his sister of January 1, 1947: "The money-kissers are everywhere, those soulless and omnipresent flies biting the still-warm bodies of fallen heroes and appropriating the victories others have won" (Mooradian 1978, p. 302).

Gorky began to drown himself in his work. The psychosexual regression presumably stimulated by the fire and the operation probably brought about a degree of unconscious guilt that forbade further enjoyment of his family and of the new critical acclaim being given to him. We hypothesize a regression back to imposture. In February, 1948, an interviewer (Clapp 1948) found him to be shy and speaking without conviction. He lied again by saying that he had attended Brown University as a young man. He complained that "there are no more songs in the field," that everyone is a "businessman."

A series of reviews of his exhibitions at Julien Levy from 1945 to 1948 were increasingly laudatory. Clement Greenberg (in O'Brien 1986) was at first quite critical. Then he proclaimed them to be "some of the best modern paintings turned out by an American" (p. 79). "Gorky has finally succeeded in discovering himself for what he is—not an artist of epochal stature, no epic past, but a lyrical, personal painter with an elegant, felicitous, and genuine delivery" (p. 79). And in 1948 he wrote: "Gorky is a complete hedonist, deeper in his hedonism than any French painter" (in O'Brien 1986 p. 219). Reiff (1977) more recently wrote that "Gorky's late painting is expressive of a richness of pathos and mood which is poignant and yet difficult to define. It is as if a certain combination of emotional ingredients, of despair, frustration, yearning, anguish, had been distilled to result in a new essence characteristic of Gorky's art and born of his peculiar tragedy" (p. 253).

In his personal life, however, Gorky could not acknowledge or digest the extent of the tragedies he was suffering during those years (de Kooning 1951). Waldman (1981) wrote that

> Gorky's terrible childhood experiences may have strengthened his will to survive his grave illness and the destruction by fire of his studio and his work, or it may ultimately have contributed to his collapse. His marriage, which had been troubled, now began to disintegrate. He had endured years of poverty and lack of recognition but he could not withstand the final event in the series of tragedies that befell him. [p. 60]

Waldman refers to the car accident in New Milford, Connecticut, in June, 1948, in a car driven by his dealer, Julien Levy. Gorky's neck was broken and his painting arm temporarily paralyzed. His moods and bad temper, his lack of trust, and his doubts about his wife were so violent that she left him in mid-July, and that was the time she took the children to her parents' home. On July 12, he hanged himself in his studio. He wrote "Goodbye My Loveds" in white chalk. Only after his death was the true value of his paintings established: they hang now in the galleries of our greatest museums.

Here ends the story of a man with an imposturous identity, often an outright liar, who appeared to be developing a well-integrated mature identity as he eventually had the courage to be authentic enough to present work that was uniquely his own. We cannot attribute his tragic suicide to later trauma alone. The later tragedies undoubtedly reactivated the earlier ones. These external events promoted an inner regression to the terrors that characterized his psychic reality all along. Although the successful imposture fueled his labors at better eventual self-integration, that very authentic self-presentation and identity might have been too much to bear. It must have symbolized a successful parricide that probably just could not be handled by the now not-so-imposturous man. As a child, he must have been just too burdened by the abandonment by his father and the deaths of those around him in the Armenian holocaust, and especially by the oedipal victories that his later successes symbolized. The meaning of the early and late tragedies then took on traumatic proportions because they dovetailed too precisely with the terrifying demons of his inner fantasies.

7

MEN MASQUERADING AS WOMEN: IMPOSTURE, ILLUSION, AND DENOUEMENT IN THE PLAY *M. BUTTERFLY*

An examination of the experience of the viewer of the play *M. Butterfly* enables us to expand our psychoanalytic understanding of a particular form of imposture: the cross-gender dressing of a man masquerading as a woman. In the play *M. Butterfly*, the experience of being duped is shared by protagonist and audience alike, exemplifying how a measure of gullibility and a readiness to be deceived are fairly universal characteristics. As we have already noted, the colluding and cooperating audience is critically important to the impostor. In this play, in a parallel process, both the duped fictional character and the audience simultaneously know and do not know the realities of gender. Art and psyche have worked harmoniously together in a dramatically gripping and psychologically compelling enactment of the "fantasy of the phallic woman" as conveyed through the illusions created by imposture.

Cross-gender imposture, one of several themes, is the most central and dramatic element in David Hwang's (1989) play,

Note: This chapter is an expanded version of an article by H. K. Gediman, "Men Masquerading as Women: Imposture, Illusion and Dénouement in the Play, 'M. *Butterfly*.'" *Psychoanalytic Psychology* 10: 469–479.

which is based on the true story of the Bernard Boursicot–Shi Pei Pu affair (see Wadler 1988). In the play, the focus of which is the Gallimard–Liling affair, René Gallimard, a French diplomat, is fooled by his male lover, the transvestite opera singer and spy, Song Liling, who posed for twenty years as a woman. A psychoanalytic understanding of the protagonist's and the audience's responses to the type of cross-gender imposture depicted in *M. Butterfly* may enhance our understanding, appreciation, and enjoyment of the play while it provides us with new perspectives on gender and sexuality. It is of particular value in increasing our understanding of those gender deceptions which authors who have studied perverse strategies and scenarios have found to be so critical in perversions (Kaplan 1991, McDougall 1980, Riviere 1929, Schreier 1992, Schreier and Libow 1993, Stoller 1975). The flagrant example of imposture in this play, of a man masquerading as a woman by cross-dressing, can illuminate and underscore many of the mysteries of imposture, deception, and perversion.

The contribution that psychoanalysis has made to understanding the success of certain kinds of imposturous caricatures in fooling others is to be found in what Freud, in 1927, referred to as the "fantasy of the phallic woman." This seminal contribution needs to be augmented by integrating it with the more recent psychoanalytic observations and conceptualizations of the fear of the vagina. It seems clear from the truths embodied in this play that the living out of this fantasy in certain guises may be regarded as one important variety of imposture. One cannot make any assumptions about the playwright's or the actors' knowledge of or intentions to portray, either consciously or unconsciously, the psychoanalytic views presented here.[1] But one can assume that the insights provided by psychoanalytic

---

1. An exception is Hwang's (1990) personal communication to Helen K. Gediman after reading an early draft in which he said: "I found your paper quite illuminating. While I can't say that I was *consciously* aware of everything you suggest, I feel your observations are valid."

thinking derive from universal wishes, fantasies, anxieties, and conflicts, which are shared communally at some level of consciousness, in the psyches of author, protagonist, actor, and audience alike. In this chapter, we elaborate on the fantasy of the phallic woman as universal and as embedded in the message of this play. To do so, we present certain updated views of gender.

The power of the play derives not only from our fascination with the psychology of imposture but also from the skillful interweaving of its plot of duplicity and domination with the similar plot in Puccini's 1900 opera, *Madame Butterfly*. The true-to-life staged spy story of Liling, the impostor, dovetails in a dramatic analogy with the actual libretto and plot of the opera. Whereas the imposture theme emerges gradually as the play's plot unfolds, parallels with the opera are drawn early on. In the opera, the relationship between Pinkerton and Butterfly is depicted as one in which the man epitomizes imperialist domination by Western nations over weak Eastern societies. Puccini's work gives particular emphasis to the counterpoint of the West as symbolized by the dominant male and the East as symbolized by the passive, submissive, demure, and helpless female. In the opera, the Eastern female, Butterfly, is enthralled with Pinkerton and his Western male domination. Ultimately, this subjugation leads to her self-destruction by means of suicide.

In Hwang's play, Gallimard is a French diplomat assigned to the People's Republic of China in 1960, when France was a world power with strong colonial interests and China was still relatively undeveloped. Gallimard meets Liling, a leading soprano in the Beijing opera, who was performing the title role of *Madame Butterfly*. This was at a time when all female roles were sung by men, but Gallimard was apparently ignorant of that fact. He enters into a long, intimate love relationship with "him," whom he assumed was "her." As a theme within a theme, Liling often tauntingly and ironically confronts Gallimard with the issue of Western domination over Asian peoples. Motifs of global politics and sexual politics are contrapuntally expressed. The second theme, which develops slowly and emerges fully only much later in the play, concerns Liling's double imposture. By cross-dressing in a blatant and evidently quite successful imperson-ation of a woman, on and off stage, and by being a spy, Liling dupes Gallimard both sexually and politically for twenty years. The sexual and gender deceptions in his perverse imposture indeed contain a heavy measure of personal power, control, and the discharge of anal sadism. This deception occurs in the con-text of political deception, deceiving that automatically attaches to acts of diplomatic counterintelligence and espionage.

Marjorie Garber (1993) devotes a chapter in her book, *Vested Interests*, to a deconstructivist analysis of Hwang's play. Although Garber attempts some psychoanalytically based analysis of cross-over and deception in the play, her approach is primarily that of well-documented literary criticism emphasizing the cultural politics of gender and transvestism. She concludes that cross-dressing such as Liling's proves that gender is constructed and not essential or innate, a view that is, for the most part, alien to psychoanalytic thinking. According to Garber, the cultural fact at the center of the fantasy in the play is "the fact of transvestism as both a personal and a political as well as an aesthetic and theatrical mode of self-construction" (1993, p. 236). What is compatible with psychoanalytic thinking in her fascinating argu-ment is the idea that acting, spying, diplomacy, transvestism, and other varieties of cross-dressing are forms of border crossing and are therefore compatible with the ideas presented here on im-posture and deception. According to Garber

> the figure of the cross-dressed "woman," the transvestite figure borrowed *both* from Chinese and Japanese stage traditions . . . functions simultaneously as a mark of gender undecidability and as an indication of category crisis. Man/woman, or male/female is the most obvious and central of the border crossings in M. Butterfly [and] . . . indicates the play's preoccupation with the transvestite as a figure not only for the conundrum of gender and erotic style, but also for other kinds of border-crossing, like *act-ing* and *spying*. [pp. 238–239]

A true impostor, as we noted earlier, is defined as one who passes himself off incognito, often in delinquent, psychopathic, sociopathic, and other criminal ways, as actually possessing an identity of someone other than himself. Song Liling, of course, did just this, in the variant of imposture known as cross-dressing and female impersonation. And his espionage certainly involved assuming an outright false identity. When the assumption of a false identity involves posing as a member of the opposite sex or gender, imposture takes on specific meaning.

As we have emphasized, almost all psychoanalytic studies of the true impostor, as well as those dealing with lesser imposturous tendencies ranging from outright lying, through mild deceptions, to playacting an identity, on or off stage, note the absolute necessity of an *audience* to the impostor. Abraham (1925) was especially aware of how the impostor requires a co-operating, colluding, gullible audience to guarantee the success of the imposture. Gallimard's self-deception indeed enabled him to fulfill this role for the doubly deceitful Liling. And in viewing the play, we as audience are also deceived. Gallimard's passion for Liling is rooted in his compassion for Puccini's Butterfly and in all of the tender, guilty, protective feelings that her domination by Western imperialism stirred up in him. The stage for the double-duping involving sexual and international politics is further set by Liling's teasing discussions with Gallimard about the sexual, racial, commercial, and political domination of East by West. And at some point during the performance, we the audience also feel teased by the playwright and actor.

The part of Liling was played, in the major production of the play that we saw, by a male actor, B. D. Wong. Wong cross-dressed imposturously in two stunning female impersonations: (1) on the operatic stage in his role of Liling singing Butterfly and (2) off the operatic stage in his role of Liling the cross-dressing impostor-spy. We, the audience, were both witness to and willing victims of the double deceptions depicted on stage so artfully and skillfully by the playwright and performers. Our gullibility thus paralleled that of Gallimard, as the various threads of the dramatized duplicity interlaced with *our* willing suspension of disbelief in the double deception. And we remained gullible despite the obviousness in the ruses of gender impersonation and espionage that were unfolding before our very eyes. Like the analyst with his or her patient, the audience of a play willingly suspends disbelief, perhaps balancing it, as the analyst does, with a healthy degree of skepticism or even measured "paranoia" about the inconsistencies in the deceptions of the drama. The latter deceptions involve *illusion*, and not the hostile attacks on the analyst's sense of reality that are characteristic of patients who lie.

Although the dramatist and performers made bold attempts to sustain the gender deception for the audience, press releases, some program notes, and published essays have prematurely exposed the facts of the imposture to many members of the audience. Whereas earlier audiences were often fooled, more recent playgoers were frequently aware of Liling's (and Wong's) gender reality. We too were gulled by the unfolding drama, though preconsciously aware from the beginning, of that which was to be gradually unraveled and finally exposed fully as bold truth during the play's most climactic and dramatic moment: the visually startling denouement of Wong-as-Liling's naked male body, previously disguised as female. Can we assume a parallel process in Gallimard, that he was aware, as we were, of the deception behind Liling's exposure of the naked truth? It is this visually traumatic exposure of two truths that Gallimard had long denied—that is, Liling's true gender and then his own (in fact homosexual) behavior—which culminates in his final mortification and suicide by the ritual disembowelment of hara-kiri. Gallimard's suicide follows a humiliating confrontation with Liling's double deception of espionage and gender, as well as the fact of his own self-deception, a confrontation with his changed self-perception, from having been the one who dominates to becoming the one who is dominated, both politically and sexually. In the opera, it is the woman, Butterfly, who commits suicide following her abject shame and grief upon hearing of Pinkerton's deception and sexual betrayal of her. We theorize that Gallimard, in his final act of self-immolation, feels totally merged as one with the "inferior," Eastern, submissive, subjugated woman, and he literally masquerades as the shamed, dishonored Madame Butterfly, as he dons the wig and kimono worn by Liling when the opera singer played that role. In this final act of self-immolation, he is united with her by becoming her, symbolically.

It is an amazing thing to be a member of the audience viewing this production, knowing in advance the very twist of plot that builds to the climactic "surprise" moment of revelation in the play's last act. Throughout the play, leading up to the denouement, at the same time that one *knows*, one *does not know*. For example, a colleague who knew of the outcome before seeing the play said that she "forgot" it totally while watching the play and was shocked by it. This simultaneous perception and disavowal of a perception must be the very psychological mechanism that enabled the protagonist, René Gallimard, to cohabit intimately with Song Liling for twenty years and not know that the opera singer was a man, not a woman. It could be said that, in the case of the playwright fooling the audience, we are in the sphere of *artifice and creativity*. In the case of Liling's duping, however, we are in the sphere of *artifice and perversion*. In the mind of every member of the audience must hover some version of the obvious question, "How could he have been Liling's lover and not know the true nature of Liling's genitals?" or, "How did Liling manage his sexual contacts so as to hide the fact of his gender?" That is, we assume that the audience's questions mirror Gallimard's and that there is a *parallel process* going on in the minds of fictionalized character and audience alike. Parallel process, in its clinical manifestations in treatment and supervision, is familiar to psychoanalysts, as we illustrated in Chapter 5. In this instance, the parallel process involving the play and its audience enables a mutual denial or disavowal of the perception of what in fact is really there. And this denial proceeds despite what must be *all the evidence of the senses*. This assumption is in fact buttressed by Hwang himself in a personal communication to Helen K. Gediman (1990) "In fact, I *did* intend for the audience to participate in the process of at once knowing Song's gender, and simultaneously denying that knowledge, thus recapitulating Gallimard's experience, as you point out so well."

In this case, what is disavowed is the presumed knowledge of the true anatomical difference between the sexes. What is in fact really there, yet is denied by Gallimard, is the presence of his lover's male genital. Therefore, the parallel, let us say illusionary experience of audience and protagonist, is that it is not *really* there. Also denied is the absence of the female genital, so that what Gallimard presumably knows is *not* there is responded to, wishfully, as though it really were there. Such illusionary experiences have long been of great interest to psychoanalysts in their attempt to elucidate many instances of overt and latent homosexuality, of fetishism, and of other forms of sexuality commonly referred to as the perversions. In all of them, but particularly in cases of men cross-dressing as women or as caricatures of women, men may convince themselves through clothing or fetishistic objects that a woman, if only an illusionary woman, does indeed possess a penis, albeit a penis whose presence is then denied, along with the denial of the fact that she does instead possess a vagina. The concretization in cross-dressing that provides the "woman" with a real penis reflects the primitive thinking of the perverse character, along with the as-if and the illusionary. Transvestism, cross-dressing, and related forms of imposture, in addition to being instances of deception generally, are variations of enactments of the fantasy of the phallic woman, a fantasy considered by Bak (1968) to be universal in the sexual perversions.

When Freud (1927) introduced the notion of the phallic woman fantasy in his work on fetishism, he noted that, at some time during their early development, all boys refuse to take cognizance of the fact that a woman does not possess a penis. "No, that could not be true," Freud said of the little boy's disavowal of this critical piece of reality, "for if a woman had been castrated, then his own possession of a penis was in danger" (1927, p. 153). The conviction that a woman has a penis "remains a token of triumph over the fear of castration and a protection against it" (p. 153). It should be noted that Freud's emphasis on the denial of the absence of the penis in women was accompanied by his ellipsis of the little boy's need to deny the presence of the vagina. Freud has been rightly criticized for neglecting this important aspect of the phallic woman fantasy, but his omission should be regarded as a consequence of his own "phallocentrism" and should be rectified in light of our current understanding of the anxieties and terrors that the positive knowledge of the female genital can evoke in very young boys. Kaplan (1991) regards Freud's *omission* both as consistent with a 4-year-old boy's anxious imaginings about gender and therefore as a use of the perverse strategy. Freud's paper on "Fetishism," she writes, is in itself a "fetishistic document" (p. 55). Although most boys outgrow this fantasy, it remains a potent organizing force in certain personalities, determining the sexual preference of some fetishistic and/or latent to overt homosexual men, as well as of certain men with heterosexual object choices. In their various enactments of the fantasy of the phallic woman, then, these men attempt to overcome persisting childhood castration fears either by masquerading as, or choosing as sexual partners, women or men masquerading as "women" who are symbolically endowed with the characteristic that makes them tolerable as sexual partners.

It is well known that a perception may be simultaneously both acknowledged and disavowed, even among the nondelusional and nonpsychotic. Cross-dressing, the case in point, prototypically permits both partners to maintain the illusion of the woman with the penis. The fantasy of the phallic woman is gratified in these conditions, insofar as something that one wishes were there but that in reality is *not* there—that is, a real male genital on a real woman—is responded to illusorily, or by various degrees of self-deception, as though in fact it really *were* there. We refer to this self-deception as the first layer of a disavowal.

Liling was one such "woman" with a penis in his imposturous caricature; thus, the imposture in this case may be understood as a variant of the fantasy of the phallic woman. When we view the play M. Butterfly from a psychoanalytic point of view, we encounter an apparent reversal of the fantasy's usual content. In what we presume to be Gallimard's unconscious fantasy life, the penis is first perceived, and then that perception is disavowed. Usually, that which is disavowed is the absence of a penis on a real woman and not, as in this case, the presence of a penis on an impersonated woman. Fetishism is the clearest case, where the fetish is the substitute for the woman's penis. We presume that the fetishist, like Gallimard, has been traumatized by the sight of the female genital as having no penis. The fetishist adds something—a piece of leather, a garter belt—filling in the gap with, as it were, a positive hallucination. Gallimard, in a reversal, subtracts something. He presumably sees no penis where there actually is one, creating a gap with something akin to a negative hallucination. Something, then, that is really present, the male genital, is responded to illusorily, by protagonist and audience alike, as though it were not there. Gallimard's psychological blind spot or negative hallucination of his lover's actual penis protects and defends against the double demons of castration and homosexuality. We might further speculate that the very blind spot that defends against castration also expresses a wish to castrate.

How well Freud understood this compromise formation in the fetishism specific to Chinese culture! He wrote, "A parallel to fetishism in social psychology, might be seen in the Chinese custom of mutilating the female foot and then revering it like a fetish after it has been mutilated. It seems as though the Chinese male wants to thank the woman for having submitted to being castrated" (1927, p. 157).

And it is as though Gallimard were saying to Liling, "You are my submissive, inferior, Chinese, Eastern lover; therefore, there is no way that you can possess a penis and its accompanying powers. Only I have that." By means of his scotomization,

Gallimard was also able to disavow the fact that his lover *did* possess a penis, and he could thereby promote the illusion that his lover was a woman and that he was not engaging in homosexual activity. In the usual version of the fantasy, the fetishistic man, for instance, or one choosing a transvestite love object, has it all—a woman with a penis—by creating in his mind a real woman with an illusory penis. In this play, the (at least latent) homosexual man has it all, as denial and tricks of imagination enable him to possess an illusory woman with a real penis.

We might take this analysis one step further and assume that Gallimard also was guided unconsciously by the universal fantasy of the phallic woman and that he was beset with castration anxiety. The play provides ample evidence of his fear of the genitally female woman and its connection with his homophobia and subsequent massive repression of his male lover's true gender. The playwright explicitly includes material delineating a personality with a lifelong history of shyness and reluctance to make contact with women. Gallimard avoided most opportunities provided by a college chum to carouse with women, with the exception of one brief date with a young and fawning American "bimbette." In his marriage, his wife complained of their having had no children. We are given to believe that the marriage had not been consummated through genital intercourse and had persisted for only practical and never sexual reasons. We wonder if Gallimard was a virgin. As suave and worldly as Gallimard was with Liling, he was shy and retiring with women from his own cultural milieu. We feel quite comfortable, then, in speculating that he was able to consummate a union with his transvestite lover only because that lover *did* have a penis, sparing him the horrifying contact with the female genitals of his persisting 4-year-old's imagination. Then, again, we might wonder if perhaps the affair were never truly consummated. Gallimard knew, but he did not know, just as the audience knew, but did not know. These parallel reactions of audience and protagonist involve a double disavowal: in order to defend against the knowledge that all women *do not* have penises—the usual version of the phallic woman fantasy, and what we earlier referred to as the first layer in Gallimard's double disavowal—our protagonist had also to disavow that his male lover-impersonating-a-woman *did* in fact have a penis, the reversal in the second layer of Gallimard's disavowal. In the artistic depiction of this double-layered disavowal lies the heart of the play's mystery and its success in engaging the audience's willingness to be fooled. The relation of the work of art portraying deception to the gullible audience that views it is similar to the relation between the deceptive patient and the gullible analyst who suspends disbelief without a counterbalancing healthy skepticism.

In general, whether the disavowed is the presence of the penis, as in *M. Butterfly*, or its absence, as in instances of fear of the vagina—that is, the simple presence or absence of the penis—is not particularly relevant for our understanding of the kind of self-deception in which Gallimard must have engaged. Most contemporary psychoanalysts would agree with Bak (1968) who believes that the fantasy of the phallic woman is ubiquitous in all perversions and that what is relevant is the *ambiguity* and *uncertainty* as to *gender*, and not simply the presence or absence of a penis. Equivocal perceptions and the lack of intimate knowledge of the female genital are responsible for the young boy's suspension of decision about the presence or absence of a penis. He remains uncertain, neither denying nor accepting his own perception, so that the question of what is more important, the absence or the presence of the penis, is a moot one. One imagines that such uncertainty persisted in Gallimard's ability to remain unknowing for some twenty years. And it is this very ambiguity of perception that is reflected in the "M." of the play's title. Although in France, "M." stands for "Monsieur," in America, it might well be the mode of address for either, any, or both genders—a unisex, leveling form of address. This is the kind of leveling that tries to obscure the differences between genders and sometimes also the generations, that characterizes the element of deception in the perversions at large.

The de facto relationship between René Gallimard and Song Liling is homosexual. The homosexuality is not to be confused with the perverse. The *fetishistic* solution for dealing with homosexual and other anxieties in both men and women constitutes the perversion. If Liling's gender had been known to Gallimard and if Gallimard had been fully conscious of his object-gender choice, the relationship would have been both homosexual and fetishistic, for from Gallimard's point of view, his lover's cross-dressing and female impersonation would be among the conditions or requirements for sexual satisfaction. Such an overt, *conscious* choice of a homosexual man who cross-dresses would, according to the psychoanalytic view just summarized, represent an enactment of the phallic woman fantasy as a way of avoiding castration anxiety. According to that view, the appearance— whether by art, artifice, illusion, by any manner of deception, or by fantasy—of the phallus or its symbolic equivalent, as in a fetish, on someone who in all other respects is *visibly* a woman, *levels* the differences between the sexes. This leveling helps eliminate the anxiety that such differences may call forth in those men, whether homosexual or heterosexual, who have not resolved childhood conflicts centering on castration anxieties. In this instance, the fetishistic solution, a perversion, is a way of dealing with homosexual anxieties via a particular route of deception in one of its important variations. It is now widely believed that such leveling and deceptive elimination of differences and distinguishing characteristics also deal with the more preoedipal anxieties of separating out of the merger with the mother of earliest childhood.

In the program notes in the *Playbill* (1988), we learn of the difficulties experienced by John Lithgow, who originally played Gallimard, and by playwright Hwang in coming to terms with the leaks to the audience through the press and by word of mouth that B. D. Wong, the actor, and Song Liling, whom he portrayed, are both men. Lithgow concludes that it was all right to reveal the plot line publicly because "even if you know the premise, there is still great excitement at seeing the information gradually disclosed." Hwang notes that by the end of the evening, only a few people still could not accept the idea that a man could live with another man for twenty years and not know that he was not a woman. He contends that the production was successful in persuading the majority of people to suspend their disbelief.

Such self-deception on the part of the audience does indeed seem to be a form of the psychopathology of everyday life, as well, as we suggested earlier in our discussions of the ubiquitous dyadic relationship of the deceiver and his or her gullible receiver, whether the latter is an analyst, an audience member, or a significant Other. In its less pathological, more adaptive, and more universal guises, self-deception may be understood as a creative transformation of perceptions related to the artifice of creativity. However, to suspend disbelief in viewing *M. Butterfly*, without the corrective of taking it all with a grain of salt, must take some doing, as the sensitive audience member cannot be fooled for too long by Wong's portrayal of Liling's vocal and verbal mannerisms. The gullible viewer might hear those speech mannerisms as typical only of the submissively and exaggeratedly feminine Asian woman, but the sophisticated listener, who hears the speech intonations as feminine, is more apt eventually to consider the patterns as manneristic and stereotypic, identifying them correctly as containing the typical innuendo of a man in drag caricaturing a woman's speech and intonations.

One may suspect, in this connection, that the playwright wrote Liling's part with the specific intention of teasing the audience, of pulling its leg. One certainly may wonder if this kind of deception is a tamed-down version of perversion, although less tamed down than when there is an absence of the element of leg-pulling. Leg-pulling is a teasing act infused with varying degrees of hostility and sadism, the purpose of which is not simply to entertain an audience but to gull that audience for purposes of the deceiver's gratifications. Many of these gratifications relate to the perverse use of the object as a thing to be manipulated and to a hostile wish to destroy the object's sense of reality. Lithgow concludes in the playbill: "The play asks how anybody can fool himself that drastically, and yet the world is full of examples of delusions that extreme" (*Playbill* 1988, p. 12). But the illusion formation that accompanies boundary crossing in cross-gender identifications is a most common normative as well as pathological phenomenon. Playful identificatory interchanges between man and woman are required for maximum sexual pleasure.[2] Innate bisexual tendencies in every man and woman enable cross-gender identifications, empathy, and playful, imaginative, illusory sexual interchange. We are dealing in our case in point with an extreme version of self-deception about gender that transcends normal creative illusion formation. However, the universality of normal illusion formation with reference to gender is most important for explaining the ubiquitous gullible reaction of audiences witnessing cross-gender impersonations.

Gender ambiguity is also central to Garber's (1993) explanation of the success of the deception of transvestites and other cross-dressers. However, our positions differ in one fundamental respect. Garber takes the hermeneutic view that ambiguities, conundrums, and undecidability in gender perception are inevitable because gender is always a *construction* or interpretation and never refers to anything constant or innate. She concludes, therefore, that both real and fictionalized individuals are gendered only in representation or performance and never in reality. Our position, on the other hand, is that the critical ambiguities are due to innate bisexuality, to empathy, and to other psychologically real capacities for cross-gender identifications.

The deconstructionist approach, as well as the hermeneutic, seems to allow gender to be defined fictitiously. Chasseguet-Smirgel (1981) calls our attention to the etymological similari-

---

2. Dr. Sheldon Bach, in this discussion of an earlier version of this chapter presented at the Division 39 meeting of the American Psychological Association, New York, April 1991 elaborated extensively on this theme.

ties between the French word, "maquiller," meaning to disguise with makeup, and the word "to make," meaning to fabricate. Similarly, the words "factitious" and "fetish" share an etymology, both referring basically to the artificial. Her position is that the anal phallus in perversion is the *epitome of fabricated objects*. The concept of the anal phallus is used as a metaphor for denying genitality, leveling, as in a homogenized anal stool, the differences between the sexes and the generations. The anal phallus also reflects the child's capacity to *create* a phallus, serving for the boy as a restoration of the fantasized castrated phallus and for the girl as a creation de novo. Those who regard gender as simply a construction would also seem to be leveling differences by denying any connection between gender and genital, between gender and vagina and penis. Clearly, there is a loss of reality in the illusion that gender can be leveled to mere construct, just as there is a loss of, if not an attack on, reality in the deceptions involved in imposture and perversions such as cross-dressing. "When the hatred of reality prevails, the subject tries to *destroy reality and to create a new one, the reality of the anal world where all differences are abolished*" (Chasseguet-Smirgel 1981, p. 525).

There does seem to be a parallelism between the structure of the deconstructionist theory of gender and the structure of the subject matter of perversion that it attempts to explain. As Kaplan (1991) has written, a fetish is designed to keep the lies hidden. The human mind achieves these various levels of *deception*, as in perceiving a woman with ordinary female genitals as phallic, for a variety of reasons. One such reason is to be found in the case of the fetishistic man's need to express and disguise his wishes to be a submissive female, which to him signifies denigration. This clinging to a false version, which is created by the fetish, may be classified as a deception. The fictitious, artificial genital serves as a model for the fetish. Among transsexuals and people seeking sex-change operations, deception is obvious in the direct lie about the nature of the biological genitals.

Within the play M. *Butterfly*, characters are baffled by the success of the sexual duplicity, and the judge at the spy trial presses for details of how the imposture was in fact carried out. But to focus on such details risks obliteration of the artifice of the imposture as well as the artistry of the playwright in conveying the subtleties of imposture and illusion to the audience. Garber (1993) notes that playwright Hwang was determined not to find out any of the disputed details of the Boursicot-Shi story, which he thought of as a "deconstructivist *Madame Butterfly*" (p. 237). Although we have no knowledge of the author's and actors' conscious or unconscious intentions in structuring the portrayals in order to achieve their effects, it would be of interest to have that information.

A psychoanalytic understanding of the simultaneous knowing and not knowing the true nature of his lover's genitals could well explain Gallimard's twenty years of cohabitation with someone he believed to be a woman, yet at the same time "knew" was only masquerading as one. Along with the audience, he saw a man before him only when clear-cut genital identity was unveiled and ambiguity was erased in the deadly climactic denouement. His lover's complete undressing and genital exposure on stage form the psychically traumatic moment for the hero and the moment of maximum dramatic shock for the already knowing audience. Knowing the facts in advance apparently mitigates little or none of the startling emotional impact of visual confrontation of the reality that had previously been denied, and the subsequent painful process of stripping away the protective, defensive disavowal and denial of the imposture. The full knowledge that he had been duped by his imposturous lover–impersonator put Gallimard in full contact, fatally, with his previously defended sense of shame and literal mortification, eventuating in his suicide by disembowelment.

It has often been said that the deception involved in the perverse strategy defends against psychosis, murderous rage, and suicidal annihilation. McDougall (1980), for example, sees the reinvented primal scene of the perverse scenario as a manic defense, preferable to madness. In that sense, deception in the perversions can be the lesser of two pathological evils. Furthermore, it would seem to be no accident that disembowelment was the chosen method of self-annihilation,[3] above and beyond the Asian traditions of suicide, such as hara-kiri or seppuku, which facilitated the choice. The bowels are internal organs, often symbolizing, for men, the inner genitals, the inner sense of one's femaleness in a universal potential for cross-gender identification. And it is the hatred of the repudiated feminine side of himself that drives a certain type of man to employ the perverse strategy in an effort at deceiving himself and others with regard to the dreaded and hated femininity. With this symbolic equation in mind, one could then conclude that it was Gallimard's hatred of those feminine aspects of his own gender identification, a hatred internalized from centuries of cultural oppression and from individual attitudes toward women resonating with developmental misconceptions about women as genitally defective, that enabled his twenty-year blindness to the blatantly deceptive disguises of the gender reality of his masquerading partner as well as the final act of deadly self-mutilation. The ridicule of the burlesque was internalized in his final act of deadening when blindness no longer served its purpose. Gallimard literally transforms himself into "Madame Butterfly," cross-dressing in her kimono and wig, the very costumes and accessories that Liling wore when he played the title role in the opera. In an identification with the aggressor who duped him, and as an expression of his own hatred of his having been successfully deceived, Gallimard becomes the cross-dressed woman and then kills her, while Liling, dressed now as a man, stares at Gallimard, now the woman, calling out, "Butterfly? Butterfly?" as Gallimard plunges the knife into his internal organs. His fate and that of Madame Butterfly were as one: to die with honor when one can no longer live with honor.

---

3. We thank Dr. Adria Schwartz for suggesting this line of interpretation.

POSTSCRIPT

Marjorie Garber's (1993) views on gender as a construct and on cross-dressing as a deconstruction of gender are typical of the deconstructionist and hermeneutic approaches. Deconstructionism and hermeneutics, disciplines that disregard the reality and truth value of all matters, including that of the actual genitals, have taken hold in the Zeitgeist for reasons that might be discerned in the following passage from Chasseguet-Smirgel (1981), even though those intellectual movements were not her subject matter in this work:

> The loss of reality in perversions is not only focussed on the female genital, but leads the whole psyche into a new dimension. We cannot call this dimension a delusion, but it can be considered as a generalized illusion. As such it is necessary to understand it for its seductive qualities not only to a limited number of patients, but to all of us, and for its implications in many aspects of culture and society. [p. 533]

Both approaches reflect trends that some would want to incorporate into current psychoanalytic theory. These theoretical strategies are at the moment quite fashionable and contribute to the contemporary Zeitgeist. Our researches into the many faces of deceit strongly suggest that these intellectual and trendy currents tend to obliterate the notion of deception, allowing as they do for many versions of the truth, with no room for the traditional psychoanalytic concepts of material reality and objective truth values against which to check shifting versions of narrative truth. That is to say, an uneasy compatibility exists between the shifting versions of the impostor's reality and the shifty identifications of the as-if personality, and their counterparts in the shifting versions of narrative truth that are a hallmark of deconstructionism and hermeneutics. We say uneasy compatibility because these analogous modes of thinking, the psychopathological and those sanctioned by contemporary institutionalized traditions, do a grave injustice to psychoanalytic facts.

If any version of the truth can be substituted for another in gender determination as in Garber's (1993) interpretation of the play, *M. Butterfly*, and there are no innate constants, no standard of truth, then it becomes easy to overlook the unmistakable presence of deception in perversions. Such lack of respect for the idea of certain immutable standards of truth has eventuated, unfortunately, in what is tantamount to a sanctioning of deception as a virtue. This outcome has permeated several fashionable social and academic movements, which many feel are riddled with fraudulence or at the very least attract fraudulently inclined pseudo-scholars. A case in point is the current attitude in the collective politically correct societal view taken vis-à-vis the problem of "gender dysphoria," a view that generates popular therapeutic strategies. Those who adopt these strategies aim to treat this complaint by adopting a sort of gender-neutral attitude in the counseling and treatment of gender-dysphoric patients, some of whom request sex-change operations. It is not at all unusual to hear therapists respond to these requests by adopting a respectful, socially and politically correct attitude that leads them—at some juncture in their interaction with the patient contemplating the removal of his penis, or her breasts and uterus —to shift the pronoun designating the individual in question from "he" to "she" or "she" to "he." They switch pronouns not just in speaking to the patient, but in speaking about the patient to colleagues or other people.

Listening, one gets the impression that certain therapists working in this area have some perverse notion of what neutrality means. They seem to be deceiving themselves that their attitude toward the patient's gender change request is neutral if they can be objective behaviorally about that request for a sex-change operation. In fact, they are not neutral at all, for by unquestioningly going along with the patient's requests, they are in fact taking sides with the patient's masochistic, psychotic, or otherwise pathological attitude toward the idea of mutilating his or her own sexual organs. Listening to such therapists, one gets the impression that they are joining in with the resistance and colluding with the patients' troubled proclamations of disturbed core gender identity. It is more likely that what the patient insists relieves his or her dysphoria is not related to what psychoanalysts of any persuasion regard as core, but is more about fluid gender identifications, about caricatures of masculinity and femininity. The therapist in such cases has, in a word, been gulled, and is fluidly going along with the patients' fluid gender constructions—most of which are caricatures and stereotypes and masquerades—rationalized as addressing and curing the dysphoria.

Something in us rebels, is jarred even before the castration or other mutilation, by the easy shift of pronouns. *It just does not ring true.* It is not what we have attempted to convey about true gender throughout this chapter, where we painstakingly refer to the true gender and the deceptive disguise of true gender throughout our exposition. But when, in ordinary parlance, we refer to an individual who has had, or even is contemplating a sex-change operation, with a pronoun that is true-gender-discordant, are we not engaging in mass social deception? When some psychoanalysts do not call castration castration, when they do not designate the medically unnecessary mastectomies and hysterectomies that are involved in sex-change operations as mutilations, all in the interest of being socially and politically correct, or being on the intellectually hip or cutting edge, are they not also engaging in social deception? What gratifications might accrue from these mutually collusive deceptions that, in defiance of psychobiological fact, sanction gender as a construct, whether intellectually, or literally by the surgeon's knife? It really does seem that some are more prone to go along with the fluid gender constructs, whereas others are more prone to outrage at the condoning and promoting of genital mutilation.

Part III

CONCLUSION

8

THE DECEPTIVE
TRANSFERENCE:
A PERVERSE DYAD

> *Every perverse enactment is based on an uncon-*
> *scious scenario, designed to fulfill the central aim of*
> *the perverse strategy, which is to keep everyone's*
> *attention focused on a deception.*
>
> —L. J. Kaplan

Throughout this book we have asked the following question: Why do patients lie to their analysts? Their lies are at cross-purposes with their stated aims in selecting such a costly and time-consuming method of treatment. Why do some patients prevent their analysts from helping them reach the goals they initially set for the treatment: an honest examination of their lives and better solutions to inner conflict?

We are now better able to understand such patients when we liken the deceptive transferences to the perverse transferences. *Deceptive patients cling to their lies as perverse patients cling to the deceptions required to maintain their perversions. Both do this at the expense of being helped.* Our omitting, lying, and imposturous patients cling desperately to their deceptions and forfeit the symptom relief and characterological change originally sought when they embarked upon treatment. The imposturous supervisee forfeits with a sham presentation the option of a genuine learning experience.

The theme that stands out and reappears in different guises throughout this book is that of the *ineluctable connection between deception and perversion*. The notion of disguise, like that of illusion, is central to the unconscious aims of those such as fetishists and cross-dressers, suffering from perversions that hide lies about gender. Disguise is also central to the unconscious aims of the analysand who masks his repudiated motivations, albeit not always with regard to gender, with deceit. Perversions always involve a deception. What we have concluded is that *deception in the analytic situation may be regarded, broadly speaking, as a perversion of the relationship between analyst and analysand and that the transference of deceptive patients can be regarded as a perverse transference*. When we use the term "perverse," we are not referring at all to any specific behavior, because any so-called perverse behavior may in some situations not be perverse at all and any so-called normal behaviors may in context be perverse. By perversion, we refer to a *strategy*, usually involving illusion formation of one sort or another, that is used to influence the Other, the audience, the "anonymous spectator" (McDougall 1980), in this case, the *analyst*. As Chasseguet-Smirgel (1981) notes, the tricks the pervert uses to fascinate us make us share for an instant his illusion that the range of possibilities has been stretched out infinitely. So, too, can the liar fascinate the analyst, who is also interested in multiple, if not infinite possibilities of understanding and interpretation. The perverse strategy and scenario are to be distinguished from the creative, artistic use of illusion and the creatively crafted scripts that, technically speaking, make use of inspirational artifice, a form of deception that is located at the higher, more adaptive end of the spectrum.

The gamut of deceptions described in this book, like the perverse strategy, distracts us from the truth. Take, for example, the perverse strategy involved in exhibitionism, which, according to Kaplan (1991), involves deception in specific ways:

> Exhibitionism, like any other perverse performance, entails the kind of sleight of hand that is every magician's stock in trade. The audience is meant to keep their eyes focused on one piece of risky business so that they will not notice that something else is being sneaked in from the magician's sleeve. While everyone is concentrating on a presumably erotic performance, what is being sneaked in are hatred and vengeance. [p. 13]

The individual who lies to the analyst, too, seeks to divert him or her from the purpose at hand, and destroys a commitment to unfettered exploration in an attack on meaning and truth.

Let us look at the more traditionally understood ways in which deception as perversion manifests itself, as in the cross-dressing and fetishism described in Chapter 7 in connection with the play, *M. Butterfly*. "What makes a perversion a perversion," writes Kaplan, "is a mental strategy that uses one or another social stereotype of masculinity and femininity in a way that deceives the onlooker about the unconscious meanings of the behaviors she or he is observing" (1991, p. 9). We need to expand the notion of gender identifications implied by masculinity and femininity to include the whole panoply of identifications with respect to gender found among imposturous and other deceptive individuals. Then we can see the similarity between the perverse and the deceptive strategies.

It seems to be quite a jump, seeing a connection between someone who intends to deceive the object of his sexual desires about the nature of his gender and someone who intends to deceive his analyst about his motives as an analysand. Yet, there are many similarities in the two dyads. If we examine the gender deceptions involved in perverse strategies or scenarios, we can deduce something very important about deception in the analytic situation. For example, it has been said that women are more prone than men to deceit because genitally, women are equipped to fake orgasm, whereas men are not. Kaplan (1991) disagrees with this stereotype, saying that orgasm trickery is supported by character development rooted in a social order. It has also been said that men are more likely than women to be true impostors, another characterization also rooted in social stereotypes, as well as in our understanding that imposture is one way that men deal with castration anxiety. It may be that impostors tend to be males with castration anxiety as a standard subtext of imposture, whereas Munchausen lying and pseudo-logia lying are more typically female. Be that as it may, those who employ the perverse strategy to deceive their significant others, and those who omit, lie, and pose in the analytic situation are masquerading as caricatures, the former as the opposite gender, the latter as analysands. In both cases, the masquer-aders engage in that deception either *to look like their idealized selves as a way of making restitution for some narcissistic defect or to hide their denigrated and repudiated selves as a way of dealing with shame and guilt.* These narcissistic injuries and emptiness had their genesis in childhood. In the cases we studied, cited in Chapters 2, 3, and 4, the parent–child relationships were frag-mented, and communication was inconsistent. There was usu-ally a history of multiple caretakers and nomadic family life, and whatever parenting there was was characterized by intermittent decathexis (Furman and Furman 1984).

A perversion involves a lie. A lie involves a perversion of the relationship with the one being lied to. Schreier's (1992) and Schreier and Libow's (1993) studies of women who suffer from Munchausen syndrome by proxy provide us with a further understanding of the connection between deception and perver-sion that is consistent with ours. The women in Schreier's sample, who lied to their doctors by protesting that they were super-mothers in nurturing their ill children, actually did serious and often fatal damage to their children as a means of maintaining a perverse connection with the children's pediatricians. These dangerous deceivers masqueraded in a good-mother role in order to maintain intense, yet distant, relationships with powerfully loved yet feared parent surrogates, the children's doctors. They are thus, like Riviere's (1929) and Kaplan's (1991) women, masquerading as women, as submissive, idealizing women, a form of deception that Kaplan believes is prototypical of the female perversions.

We, along with Schreier (1992), McDougall (1980), Kaplan (1991), and Stoller (1995), believe that not only are the deceptive perversion and the perverse deception understandable as motivated defenses or compromises in the psychic economy but, in their more *severe* manifestations, they may also defend against even worse pathology of a psychotic core, characterized by unbridled murderous rage and aggression. This is so because deceptions usually derive from traumatic roots and profoundly disturbed structural development. As Schreier rightly comments, "Perversions, however onerous, are a small price to pay to deny the terrors and mortifications of childhood trauma" (1992, p. 429). And, we might add, deceptions are a small price to pay, at least psycho-economically speaking, from the point of view of some of the adult deceivers who might otherwise have gone over the edge into frank psychosis.

GULLIBILITY AND THE DYAD

Gullibility manifests itself in the psychoanalytic situation in two major forms. In the first, the analyst senses that the patient is being deceived, usually with regard to finances or amorous infidelities, by a significant person in his or her life, as discussed in Chapter 3. The patient, in these cases, generally engages in massive denial and other forms of self-deception in order to avoid whatever anxiety would have to be mastered were he or she to face squarely what is happening, which could possibly involve a threat of major loss of both the object and of self-esteem.

In the second instance, the analyst is gulled by a patient with significant psychopathic or other imposturous tendencies, or in the case of less severely disturbed patients, the analyst is lied to or presented with information with significant omissions. Many of these latter patients wish to falsify reality in order to make it more palatable or must resort to extreme denial for defensive purposes. In both cases, the analyst is confronted with the task of dealing with gullibility—the patients' or his or her own. In both cases, narcissistic issues in the patient become central determinants of dosage, timing, and tact in the confrontation of the lie, to say nothing of the subsequent interpretation of its dynamic and genetic meanings. Several issues, especially, again, narcissistic ones, are important determinants in the analyst's own understanding and use of the countertransference, whether induced, as it often is in these cases, or stemming from the analyst's own unresolved personal transferences toward patients by whom he or she feels deceived.

As for the transference–countertransference interaction between guller and gulled, deceiver and deceived, there is a very special, frequently occurring pattern noted by psychoanalysts who have worked with patients who lie or otherwise deceive. These analysts find themselves pulled into enactments, however transitorily with these patients in ways they are not with their other patients. Chasseguet-Smirgel (1981) describes a fetishistic patient who told his female analyst that he had used session time to cheat on his wife with his mistress. His aim was to lure the analyst into assuming the role of the mother of his childhood, who was his accomplice in defeating any father figure's role as authority; his analyst used her awareness of the pull into this enactment to help formulate interpretations designed to reconstruct the past and to foster insights. This patient's mother would always help him fool his examiners. Both mother and son attributed ideological reasons to their deceptions, as did the imposturous man, Mr. Green, discussed in Chapter 4, whose modus operandi was to play innocent and to fool the authorities. In this pattern of deception in the analytic situation, one should have every reason to assume that the analyst would expect to be treated in the same way as all other authorities, and would not be fooled like the others. However, this is often not the case. Despite all knowledge of how patients repeat, and despite their wisdom to take care in not regarding themselves as different from people in general, as the exceptions, analysts are nonetheless vulnerable to being fooled, duped, and gulled by certain types of deceptive patients. Chasseguet-Smirgel states, "For various structural and countertransferential reasons, the analyst may be more or less an accomplice of his analysand's devious steps, and may carry out with him a *pseudoanalysis*, never reaching the depressive core which must eventually be uncovered through the loss of illusion, together with the truth in its terrible nakedness" (p. 511). This pattern is similar, whether the subject of our investigation is the interaction of trusting patient with deceiving significant Other or trusting analyst with deceptive patient.

Meloy (1988) gets to the heart of the matter in noting that those who are particularly vulnerable to the affective stimulation of the psychopath include individuals who deny their narcissistic investments and consciously perceive themselves as *helpers* endowed with *special* amounts of altruism. The psychopath, or other type of deceptive patient, often is able to read his or her analyst–helper's needs in an uncanny manner, inducing certain caretaking and altruistic countertransferences. The process generally takes place on an unconscious level. Meloy (1988) suggests that mental health professionals are particularly vulnerable to manipulation by the psychopath when the dyadic interaction concerns their competency, adequacy as helpers, or knowledge: "They are feeding your ego at the same time that they are trapping you" (p. 130). Those who consistently deny such narcissistic investments are particularly susceptible to being deceived by such individuals in the psychoanalytic situation.

GULLIBILITY OUTSIDE
THE ANALYTIC ENCOUNTER

We now turn to an example of deception in an extra-clinical situation that does not fall into either of the two categories, patient with significant other or patient with analyst, but nonetheless is quite relevant to this discussion. This "deception" and the reactions to it occurred in events taking place in the psychoanalytic world at large and involved several well-known psychoanalysts and their interactions within broader institutional and organizational contexts. Although the now infamous incident of Jeffrey Masson's relationship with the board of directors of the Sigmund Freud Archives, headed by Kurt Eissler, was seized upon by the press (Gediman 1985b) in its attempt to galvanize and titillate the public's interest in potential shame and scandal in the psychoanalytic "family," the facts of the case stand as a prime example of the sociopsychological dynamics of a dyad involving deception and the ways in which the parties to the deception eventually resolved their involvement in a painful interaction. Much can be learned from this encounter that can be applied to our understanding of the dyadic interactions of deception encountered in the psychoanalytic situation.

The phenomenon of imposture and seductive deception in psychoanalysis is central to Jeffrey Masson's relation with the Sigmund Freud Archives,[1] and of his 1984 book, *The Assault on Truth: Freud's Suppression of the Seduction Theory*. Masson essentially called Freud a liar, one who withheld evidence that disproved his later theories. The press coverage of Freud's abandonment of the seduction theory and the alleged "seducibility" of those members of the board of the Sigmund Freud Archives who at first respected and later, when they felt he had been trying to gull them, rejected Masson as Archives Project Director, polemicized some of the subtlest areas of our theory and practice. This falsification of the facts in news reporting paralleled the deceptions involved in the very incident being reported. Of particular interest is Janet Malcolm's book *In the Freud Archives* (1984). Despite her painstaking efforts at accurate reporting,

---

1. The material presented here on this controversy is an expanded version of an article by Helen K. Gediman published in the *Newsletter* of The American Psychoanalytic Association in 1985, Volume 19, Number 2.

Malcolm insufficiently credited Freud and his followers with due appreciation of a *real* world of sadness, pain, misery, and cruelty. Either unwittingly, or by lacking the knowledge of psychoanalytic subtleties with regard to seduction, she deceived the public somewhat differently from the way that Masson, her journalistic target, did by deliberately misrepresenting the psychoanalytic view of the realities of real abuse of children and others. In her book, she portrayed Masson as a character similar to the imposturous patients described in Chapter 4, as one who quickly tired of and decathected individual people and particular fields of study—Sanskrit, psychoanalysis—once they no longer served his shifting interests. A libel suit followed, in which Masson accused Malcolm of misrepresentation.

Masson, portrayed rightly or wrongly by Malcolm as surviving by such an easy substitutability of objects and interests, may have "seduced," at one time or another, some of the world's most respected psychoanalysts, including those entrusted with the Sigmund Freud Archives. No one is entirely immune from psychic trauma, or from being seduced, or from experiencing the strong reactions that inevitably follow upon the knowledge that one has been deceived or gulled. As we have said, analysts may be vulnerable to being fooled in particular ways. Analysis involves a shifting of focus, back and forth, for both parties, between the reality of the inner life to the reality of the outer world. In the course of analysis, versions of life histories change again and again. Thus, what makes for vulnerability to being fooled, deceived, and gulled may also constitute a most valuable analytic tool. It bears repeating that the corrective for this vulnerability is the adoption of the opposite attitude, a healthy skepticism. But, for the moment, we turn our focus of attention to the vulnerability to deception so paradoxically linked with analytic skill.

Those who ego syntonically display in obvious ways their infantile omnipotence may exercise a powerful attraction on certain others who are either characterologically or transitorily gullible, and on those who have renounced their own omnipotence yet who, on precisely that account, may be particularly prone to idealizing those who have not. One reason that analysts allow themselves to be lied to is because they sometimes vicariously identify with the one who indulges his or her wishes ego syntonically by lying. This identification goes beyond the delicate balance of simply entering into the patient's fantasy while maintaining an objective hold on reality, a balance we expect in all analytic endeavors. The dynamics of lying and gullibility have a very special relation to indulgence and renunciation. And if it is orality, anal sadism, sadomasochism, aggression, omnipotence, or anything at all that is indulged by one, the deceiver, and renounced by the other, the deceived one, we approach the interactional dynamics of gullibility from a developmental as well as from a here and now in the transference perspective. One may also be particularly vulnerable in states of lonely and isolated creativity, just as Freud was when he was taken in by Fliess, of being in love, or in craving immortality in the search for one's replacement. Eissler, of the Freud Archives, might have been seeking immortality in a search for his replacement, as is nearly universally so in such cases, when he was gulled by Masson whom he had trusted. The subjective experience of sudden realization, reminiscent of the shock of the traumatic moment in that real trauma that Masson falsely claimed psychoanalysis has neglected, and the subsequent process of "de-idealization"— what Malcolm correctly understands as a typical after-reaction of a *universal tendency to deny painful reality*—may also be located on the continuum ranging from the psychopathology of everyday life to the overwhelming of the ego. Ironically, one may experience such realizations and shock as fresh trauma: that is, as having been *traumatically seduced* into being fooled.

Eissler may have needed Masson, as we all may at critical times in life long for in the Other that omnipotence that we have renounced more or less successfully. This need is especially strong for those who must work intensively with the willing suspension of disbelief for reasonably long periods of time, in exploring the unknown and the ambiguous in ourselves and others.

Such yearnings constitute transitory and reversible experiential states among the otherwise resilient and sturdy, a truth well known to psychoanalysts.

The upshot of the Eissler-Masson-Malcolm episode was not so very unfortunate, ultimately, for the Freud Archives are alive, well, and thriving. Masson has published a well-received analysis of the Freud-Fliess correspondence, and analysts and the public at large have been enlightened and informed as to the complicated nature not just of real trauma, but of deception, which itself can bring on temporary traumatic states.

THE ATTACK ON REALITY

Returning now, from extra-clinical gullibility to gullibility in the psychoanalytic dyad, we amplify some of the ideas developed thus far on the attacks on meaning and on analysts' sense of reality inherent in patients' attempts to deceive them. Those writing about the perverse transference tend to see the attack on the analyst's sense of reality by the perverse patient as an anal sadistic leveling of meaningful differences between the sexes and the generations. Similar attacks by deceptive patients seem to have similar meanings. Lying to the analyst, assuming he or she is fair game for deception, is tantamount to treating the analyst psychically as a part object, as something mechanical and without worth, or as fecal matter to be manipulated and played with.

The assault on the analyst's sense of reality by the deceptive patient is reminiscent of *gaslighting* (see Calef and Weinshel 1981, Gediman 1991). The colloquial term *gaslighting* derives from the movie, *Gaslight* (1944), in which the husband, played by Charles Boyer, tries to drive his wife, played by Ingrid Bergman, crazy by shaking her confidence in her own perceptions of the level of brightness of the gaslights in the house. He alters the level, making them dimmer or brighter, and she remarks on the change. He, with a conscious and deliberate intent to have her believe she is crazy, patronizingly tells her that

the brightness level remains constant and that she only imagines, in her presumably demented mind, that it has shifted. In
the analytic dyad, similarly, the deceptive patient lies about
something that the analyst knows to be true, as in the case, described in Chapter 3, of Miss Alexander who came to her session in a taxi cab. She lied that she had walked in the rain, but
the analyst's sense of that truth was momentarily suspended
despite her having seen her emerge in a dry raincoat, sheltered
by the doorman's umbrella, in favor of the deliberately altered
version presented by the patient.

It would be of interest to us in the future to study the cues
that liars use that enable them to select recipients of their lies,
to understand how they sniff out their alter, their counterpart,
their flip side. Unconsciously, their motivations may be similar, but the net effects are opposite—one is the flip side of the
other. That is to say, the drive-related pleasure is accompanied
by anxiety and defended against in the gulled, who can only
experience gratifications by vicariously and unconsciously identifying with the one who gulls. A different side of the conflict
emerges for the guller, whose ego defects and superego lacunae
permit access to direct gratification and not simply the indirect
and vicarious gratification that the gulled experiences unconsciously. In these situations, there seems to be a basic boundary
fluidity of self and object. Khron's (1974) concept of borderline
empathy, in which there is sensitivity to the unconscious but
not to the integrated ego aspects of the other, seems useful here.
One might ask whether such cues operate in the choice of analyst.
The liar's contempt for his analyst–victim is that of someone "in
the know" for someone he or she often perceives as "out of it."

SUMMARY

Good analytic listening requires the *willing suspension of disbelief*. This stance, an adaptive transformation of gullibility, enables analysts to become sensitive to the inner reality of their

patients' experience and to respect the occurrence of real pain and trauma above and beyond fantasy. Disbelief is suspended with respect to the realities of abuses suffered in childhood. When it comes to sensitivity to omissions, lying, imposture, and the other forms of deception that enter into the dyad, however, it is equally important that we balance our willing *suspension* of disbelief with an *assumption of a measured degree of disbelief*, an adaptive transformation of suspicion and paranoia. These two basic requirements of good analytic listening should serve us well in maximizing sensitivity while ensuring against gullibility in the dyad of the analytic situation.

REFERENCES

Abraham, K. (1925). The history of an impostor in the light of psychoanalytical knowledge. *Clinical Papers in Psychoanalysis*, vol. 2:291–305. New York: Basic Books, 1955.

Arlow, J. (1969a). Unconscious fantasy and disturbances of conscious experience. *Psychoanalytic Quarterly* 38:1–27.

——— (1969b). Fantasy, memory, and reality testing. *Psychoanalytic Quarterly* 38:28–51.

——— (1971). Character perversion. In *Currents in Psychoanalysis*, ed. I. M. Marcus, pp. 317–366. New York: International Universities Press.

Bach, S. (1994). *The Language of Perversion and the Language of Love*. Northvale, NJ: Jason Aronson.

Bak, R. C. (1968). The phallic woman: the ubiquitous fantasy in perversions. *Psychoanalytic Study of the Child* 23:15–36. New York: International Universities Press.

Baker, R. (1994). Psychoanalysis as a lifeline: a clinical study of a transference perversion. *International Journal of Psycho-Analysis* 75: 743–753.

Balter, L. (1994). Why people experience art as reality: on the aesthetic illusion. Paper presented at the December meetings of the American Psychoanalytic Association, New York City.

Bellak, L., Hurvich, M., and Gediman, H. K. (1973). *Ego Functions in Schizophrenics, Neurotics, and Normals.* New York: Wiley.

Bion, W. (1959). Attacks on linking. *International Journal of Psycho-Analysis* 40:308–315.

Blum, H. (1983). The psychoanalytic process and analytic inference: A clinical study of a lie and a loss. *International Journal of Psycho-Analysis* 64:17–33.

Bok, S. (1978). *Lying: Moral Choice in Public and Private Life.* New York: Pantheon.

Bollas, C. (1987). *The Shadow of the Object.* New York: Columbia University Press.

Calef, V., and Weinshel, E. (1981). Some clinical consequences of introjection: gaslighting. *Psychoanalytic Quarterly* 50:44–67.

Chasseguet-Smirgel, J. (1981). Loss of reality in perversions—with special reference to fetishism. *Journal of the American Psychoanalytic Association* 29:511–534.

Clapp, T. P. (1948). Arshile Gorky. *The Waterbury Sunday Republican Magazine*, February 9.

Conrad, S. E. (1975). Imposture as a defense. In *Tactics and Techniques in Psychoanalytic Therapy*, vol. 2, ed. P. L. Giovacchini, pp. 413–426. New York: Jason Aronson.

——— (1957). Review of E. Schwabacher, "Arshile Gorky." *Saturday Review*: 50, 52:16–17.

de Kooning, E. (1951). Gorky: painter of his own legend. *Art News*, January.

de Paulo, B. M., Jordan, A., Irvine, A., and Laser, P. S. (1982). Age changes in the detection of deception. *Child Development* 53:701–709.

Deutsch, H. (1923). Pathological lying (abs.). *International Journal of Psycho-Analysis* 4:159.

——— (1942). Some forms of emotional disturbances and their relationship to schizophrenia. In *Neuroses and Character Types*, pp. 262–281. New York: International Universities Press, 1965.

——— (1955). The impostor: contribution to ego psychology of a type of psychopath. In *Neuroses and Character Types*, pp. 318–338. New York: International Universities Press, 1965.

——— (1964). Some clinical considerations of the ego ideal. *Journal of the American Psychoanalytic Association* 12:512–521.

Dietrich, D. R. (1990). *Childhood object loss, the lost immortal parent complex, and mourning.* Presented at The American Psychological Association, Boston, August.

Doren, D. M. (1987). *Understanding and Treating the Psychopath.* New York: Wiley.

Eidelberg, J. (1938). Pseudo-identification. *International Journal of Psycho-Analysis* 19:321–330.

Eisenstadt, M., Haynal, A., Rentchnick, P., and de Senarclens, P. (1989). *Parental Loss and Achievement.* New York: International Universities Press.

Ekstein, R., and Caruth, E. (1972). Keeping secrets. In *Tactics and Techniques in Psychoanalytic Therapy,* ed. P. L. Giovacchini, pp. 200–218. New York: Science House.

Erikson, E. H. (1959). *Identity and the Life Cycle.* Psychological Issues, Monograph 1. New York: International Universities Press.

——— (1968). *Identity: Youth and Crisis.* New York: Norton.

Etchegoyen, H. (1991). *The Fundamentals of Psychoanalytic Technique.* London: Karnac.

Farber, L. H. (1975). Lying on the couch. *Salmagundi* 29:15–27.

Feldman, M. C., and Ford, C. V., with Reinhold, T. (1994). *Patient or Pretender: Inside the Strange World of the Factitious Disorders.* New York: Wiley.

Fenichel, O. (1928). On isolation. In *Collected Papers of Otto Fenichel,* ed. H. Fenichel and D. Rapaport, first series, pp. 147–152. New York: Norton, 1954.

——— (1939). The economics of pseudologia fantastica. In *The Collected Papers of Otto Fenichel,* ed. H. Fenichel and D. Rapaport, second series, pp. 129–140. New York: Norton, 1954.

Finkelstein, L. (1974). The impostor: aspects of his development. *Psychoanalytic Quarterly* 43:85–114.

——— (1989). Private communication to Janice S. Lieberman.

Fogel, G. I. (1991). Perversity and the perverse: updating a psychoanalytic paradigm. In *Perversions and Near Perversions in Clinical Practice,* ed. G. I. Fogel, pp. 1–16. New Haven: Yale University Press.

Ford, C. V., King, B. H., and Hollender, M. H. (1988). Lies and liars: psychiatric aspects of prevarication. *American Journal of Psychiatry* 145:554–562.

Freud, A. (1946). *The Ego and the Mechanisms of Defense.* New York: International Universities Press.

Freud, S. (1908 [1907]). Creative writers and daydreaming. *Standard Edition* 9:141–153.

———— (1909). Notes on a case of obsessional neurosis. *Standard Edition* 10:153–249.

———— (1913). Two lies told by children. *Standard Edition* 12:305–310.

———— (1915). Instincts and their vicissitudes. *Standard Edition* 14:117–140.

———— (1916). Some character types met with in psychoanalytic work. *Standard Edition* 14:311–336.

———— (1920). The psychogenesis of a case of homosexuality in a woman. *Standard Edition* 18:146–220.

———— (1921). Group psychology and the analysis of the ego. *Standard Edition* 18:67–143.

———— (1927) Fetishism. *Standard Edition* 21:149–157.

———— (1937). Constructions in analysis. *Standard Edition* 23:256–269.

———— (1938/1940). Splitting of the ego in the process of defense. *Standard Edition* 23:271–278.

Furman, E., and Furman, J. (1984). Intermittent decathexis: a type of parental dysfunction. *International Journal of Psycho-Analysis* 65:423–434.

Garber, M. (1993). *Vested Interests.* New York: HarperCollins.

Gediman, H. K. (1983). Review of R. S. Wallerstein, "On Becoming a Psychoanalyst: A Study of Psychoanalytic Supervision." *Review of Psychoanalytic Books* 2:415–428.

———— (1985a). Imposture, inauthenticity, and feeling fraudulent. *Journal of the American Psychoanalytic Association* 33:911–935.

———— (1985b). Point of view: psychic trauma and the press. *American Psychoanalytic Association Newsletter* 19: (2)1, 3–5.

———— (1986). The plight of the imposturous candidate: learning amidst the pressures and pulls of power in the institute. *Psychoanalytic Inquiry* 6:67–91.

———— (1989). Conflict and deficit models of psychopathology: a unificatory point of view. In *Self Psychology: Comparisons and Contrasts,* ed. D. W. Detrick and S. Detrick. Hillsdale, NJ: Analytic Press.

———— (1990). Men masquerading as women: imposture, illusion, and denouement in the play *M. Butterfly. Psychoanalytic Psychology* 10:469–479.

———— (1991). Seduction trauma: complemental intrapsychic and interpersonal perspectives on fantasy and reality. *Psychoanalytic Psychology* 8:381–401.

Gediman, H. K., and Wolkenfeld, F. (1980). The parallelism phenomenon in psychoanalysis and supervision: its reconsideration as a triadic system. *Psychoanalytic Quarterly* 49:234–255.

Giovacchini, P. (1985). An analyst at work: reflections. In *Analysts at Work*, ed. J. Reppen, pp. 1–26. Hillsdale, NJ: Analytic Press.

Gottdiener, A. (1982). The impostor: an interpersonal point of view. *Contemporary Psychoanalysis* 18:438–454.

Greenacre, P. (1945). Conscience in the psychopath. *American Journal of Orthopsychiatry* 15:495–509.

——— (1954). The role of transference: practical considerations in relation to psychoanalytic therapy. In *Emotional Growth. Psychoanalytic Studies of the Gifted and a Great Variety of Other Individuals,* vol. 2, pp. 627–640. New York: International Universities Press, 1971.

——— (1958a). The impostor. In *Emotional Growth. Psychoanalytic Studies of the Gifted and a Great Variety of Other Individuals,* vol. 1, pp. 193–212. New York: International Universities Press, 1971.

——— (1958b). The relation of the impostor to the artist. In: *Emotional Growth. Psychoanalytic Studies of the Gifted and a Great Variety of Other Individuals,* vol. 2, pp. 533–554. New York: International Universities Press, 1971.

Greenson, R. (1967). *The Technique and Practice of Psychoanalysis.* New York: International Universities Press.

Grossman, L. (1993). The perverse attitude toward reality. *Psychoanalytic Quarterly* 62:422–436.

Hanly, C. (1990). The concept of truth in psychoanalysis. *International Journal of Psycho-Analysis* 71:375–384.

Hwang, D. H. (1989). *M. Butterfly.* New York: New American Library.

——— (1990). Personal communication to Helen K. Gediman.

Isaacs, K. S., Alexander, J., and Haggard, E. A. (1963). Faith, trust, and gullibility. In *The World of Emotions: Clinical Studies of Affect and Their Experience,* ed. C. Socarides, pp. 355–375. New York: International Universities Press.

Jacobson, E. (1964). *The Self and the Object World.* New York: International Universities Press.

Kaplan, L. J. (1989). *The Family Romance of the Impostor-Poet Thomas Chatterton.* Berkeley: University of California Press.

———— (1991). *Female Perversions: The Temptations of Emma Bovary.* New York: Doubleday.

Karp, D. R. (1982). *Arshile Gorky: The language of art.* Ph.D. dissertation, University of Pennsylvania.

Kernberg, O. (1975). *Borderline Conditions and Pathological Narcissism.* New York: Jason Aronson.

———— (1992). Psychopathic, paranoid, and depressive transferences. *International Journal of Psycho-Analysis* 73:3–28.

Khron, A. (1974). Borderline "empathy" and differentiation of object representations: a contribution to the psychology of object relations. *International Journal of Psychoanalytic Psychotherapy* 3:142–165.

Kohut, H. (1971). *The Analysis of the Self.* New York: International Universities Press.

Kovar, L. (1975). The pursuit of self-deception. *Salmagundi* 29:28–44.

Kris, E. (1956). The personal myth: a problem in psychoanalytic technique. *Journal of the American Psychoanalytic Association* 4:653–681.

Kursh, C. (1971). The benefits of poor communication. *Psychoanalytic Review*, 58:189–208.

Kuspit, D. (1987). Arshile Gorky: images in support of the invented self. In *The New Subjectivism: Art in the 1980s*, pp. 199–216. New York: Da Capo, 1993.

Lader, M. R. (1985). *Gorky.* New York: Abbeville.

LaFarge, L. (1994). Transferences of deceit. Paper presented at the Association for Psychoanalytic Medicine, New York, October 4.

Langs, R. (1980). Truth therapy/lie therapy. *International Journal of Psycho-Analysis* 8:3–34.

LeCarré, J. (1983). *The Little Drummer Girl.* New York: Knopf.

Lewis, M., and Saarni, C., eds. (1993). *Lying and Deception in Everyday Life.* New York: Guilford.

Lieberman, J. S. (1988). The gullibility of the analyst and the patient. Paper presented at Division 39, American Psychological Association, San Francisco, February.

———— (1991a). Arshile Gorky: from identity confusion to identity synthesis. Paper presented at Division 39, American Psychological Association, Chicago, April, and at the New York Freudian Society, January.

———— (1991b). Technical, structural, and countertransference issues with patients who lie. Paper presented at the 37th Congress of the International Psychoanalytic Association, Buenos Aires, August.

——— (1993a). What's missing in this picture? An analysis of the analysand's omissions. Paper presented at Division 39, American Psychological Association, New York, April.

——— (1993b). Omissions in psychoanalytic treatment: Structural, dynamic and technical issues. Paper presented at the 38th Congress of the International Psychoanalytic Association, Amsterdam, July.

——— (1995). Review of *Lying and Deception in Everyday Life*, eds. M. Lewis and C. Saarni; of D. Nyberg, *The Varnished Truth: Truth-Telling and Deceiving in Ordinary Life;* and of M. C. Feldman and C. V. Ford, with T. Reinhold (1994), *Patient and Pretender: Inside the Strange World of Factitious Disorders. Psychoanalytic Books* 6: 401–403.

Lipton, E. (1991). The analyst's use of clinical data and other issues of confidentiality. *Journal of the American Psychoanalytic Association* 39:967–986.

Loewald, H. (1979). The waning of the Oedipus complex. *Journal of the American Psychoanalytic Association* 27:751–776.

Machiavelli. (1514). *The Prince.* Middlesex, England: Penguin Books, 1983.

Mack Brunswick, R. (1943). The accepted lie. *Psychoanalytic Quarterly* 12:458–464.

Malcolm, J. (1983). Annals of scholarship: psychoanalysis I & II. *The New Yorker,* December 5 and 12.

——— (1984). *In the Freud Archives.* New York: Knopf.

Mamet, D. (1987). *House of Games.* New York: Grove.

Mann, T. (1936). "The Confessions of Felix Krull." In *Death in Venice and Seven Other Stories.* New York: Vintage, 1955.

Marcos, L. (1972). Lying: a particular defense met in psychoanalytic therapy. *American Journal of Psychoanalysis* 32:195–202.

Masson, J. (1984). Freud and the seduction theory. *Atlantic,* February, 253 (2):33–55.

——— (1984). *The Assault on Truth: Freud's Suppression of the Seduction Theory.* New York: Farrar, Straus, & Giroux.

McDougall, J. (1980). *Plea for a Measure of Abnormality.* London: Free Association Books. (originally published in New York: International Universities Press).

Meloy, J. R. (1988). *The Psychopathic Mind: Origins, Dynamics and Treatment*. Northvale, NJ: Jason Aronson.

Mooradian, K. (1955). Arshile Gorky. *The Armenian Review* 8:2–30.

———— (1967). The unknown Gorky. *Art News* 32, September.

———— (1971). Arshile Gorky. *Armenian Digest* September-October.

———— (1978). *Arshile Gorky Adoian*. Chicago: Gilgamesh Press, Ltd.

Moore, B. E., and Fine, B. D. (1990). *Psychoanalytic Terms and Concepts*. New Haven: The American Psychoanalytic Association and Yale University Press.

Nevelson, L. (1976). *Dawns and Dusks: Conversations with Diane MacKown*. New York: Charles Scribner's Sons.

Nin, A. (1959). *A Spy in the House of Love*. New York: Bantam, 1982.

Nyberg, D. (1993). *The Varnished Truth: Truth-Telling and Deceiving in Ordinary Life*. Chicago: University of Chicago Press.

O'Brien, J., ed. (1986). *Clement Greenberg: The Collected Papers and Criticism II. Arrogant Purpose 1945–1949*. Chicago: University of Chicago Press.

Olden, C. (1941). About the fascinating effect of the narcissistic personality. *American Imago* 2:347–355.

O'Shaughnessy, E. (1990). Can a liar be psychoanalyzed? *International Journal of Psycho-Analysis* 71:187–196.

Peterson, C., Peterson, J. L., and Sieto, D. (1983). Developmental changes in ideas about lying. *Child Development* 54:1529–1535.

Piaget, J. (1965). *The Moral Judgment of the Child*. New York: Free Press.

Playbill for *M. Butterfly*. (1988).

Poland, W. (1985). At work. In *Analysts at Work*, ed. J. Reppen, pp. 145–164. Hillsdale, NJ: Analytic Press.

Pollock, G. W. (1989). *The Mourning-Liberation Process, I & II*. New York: International Universities Press.

Random House American Dictionary. (1967). New York: Random House.

Rangell, L. (1980). *The Mind of Watergate: An Exploration of the Compromise of Integrity*. New York: Norton.

Reed, G. (1994). *Transference Neurosis and Psychoanalytic Experience*. New Haven: Yale University Press.

Reiff, R. F. (1977). A stylistic analysis of Arshile Gorky's art from 1943–1948. Ph.D. dissertation, Columbia University.

Renik, O. (1992). Use of the analyst as a fetish. *Psychoanalytic Quarterly* 61:542–563.

Riesenberg-Malcolm, R. (1989). "As-if: the phenomenon of not learning." Paper presented at the 36th Congress of the International Psychoanalytic Association, Rome, Italy, August.

—— (1990). 'As-if': the phenomenon of not learning. *International Journal of Psycho-Analysis* 71:385–392.

Riviere, J. (1929). Womanliness as a masquerade. *International Journal of Psycho-Analysis* 10:303–313.

—— (1936). A contribution to the psychoanalysis of the negative therapeutic reaction. *International Journal of Psycho-Analysis* 17:304–320. Also in *The Evolution of Psychoanalytic Technique*, eds. M. S. Bergmann and F. R. Hartmann, pp. 414–429. New York: Basic Books, 1976.

Rose, B. (1986). *Twentieth Century American Painting*. New York: Spira/ Rizzoli.

Rosenberg, H. (1962). *Arshile Gorky: The Man, The Time, The Idea*. New York: Horizon.

—— (1964). *The Anxious Object: Art Today and its Audience*. New York: Horizon.

Rosenfeld, H. (1987). *Impasse and Interpretation*. London: Tavistock.

Ross, N. (1967). The "as-if" concept. *Journal of the American Psychoanalytic Association* 15:59–82.

Sandler, I. (1970). *The Triumph of American Painting: A History of Abstract Expressionism*. New York: Harper and Row.

Sandler, J., and Sandler, A. M. (1987). The past unconscious, the present unconscious, and the vicissitudes of guilt. *International Journal of Psycho-Analysis* 68:331–342.

Saxe, L. (1991). Lying: thoughts of an applied social psychologist. *American Psychologist* 46:409–415.

Schafer, R. (1968). *Aspects of Internalization*. New York: International Universities Press.

—— (1976). *A New Language for Psychoanalysis*. New Haven: Yale University Press.

Schreier, H. A. (1992). The perversion of mothering: Munchausen syndrome by proxy. *Bulletin of the Menninger Clinic* 56:421–437.

Schreier, H. A., and Libow, J. A. (1993). *Hurting for Love: Munchausen by Proxy Syndrome*. New York: Guilford.

Schwabacher, E. (1951). *Arshile Gorky Memorial Exhibition*. New York: Whitney Museum of American Art.

Searles, H. (1986). *My Work with Borderline Patients*. New York: Jason Aronson.

Slakter, E., ed. (1987). *Countertransference*. Northvale, NJ: Jason Aronson.

Steiner, J. (1985). Turning a blind eye: the cover-up for Oedipus. *International Review of Psycho-Analysis* 12:161–172.

Stoller, R. (1975). *Perversions: The Erotic Form of Hatred*. New York: Pantheon.

Tausk, V. (1933). On the origin of the "influencing machine" in schizophrenia. In *The Psychoanalytic Reader*, ed. R. Fliess, pp. 31–64. New York: International Universities Press, 1948.

Teitelbaum, S. H. (1990). Supertransference: the role of the supervisor's blind spots. *Psychoanalytic Psychology* 7:243–258.

Thomas, D. M. (1981). *The White Hotel*. New York: Viking.

Tomkins, C. (1988). *Post-to-Neo—The Art World of the 1980's*. New York: Penguin.

Viederman, M. (1990). Edvard Munch: a life in art. Presentation to the Association for Psychoanalytic Medicine, New York, March 6.

Wadler, J. (1988). For the first time, the real-life models for Broadway's "M. Butterfly" tell of their very strange romance. *People* 30: 6, p. 91.

Waldman, D. (1981). *Arshile Gorky (1904–1948), Retrospective*. New York: Abrams.

Wallerstein, R. S., ed. (1981). *Becoming a Psychoanalyst: A Study of Psychoanalytic Supervision*. New York: International Universities Press.

Weinshel, E. M. (1979). Some observations on not telling the truth. *Journal of the American Psychoanalytic Association* 27: 503–532.

Winnicott, D. W. (1947). Hate in the countertransference. In *Through Paediatrics to Psychoanalysis*, Chapter 15. New York: Basic Books, 1975.

——— (1960). Ego distortion in terms of true and false self. In *The Maturational Processes and the Facilitating Environment*, pp. 140–152. New York: International Universities Press, 1965.

Wolff, G. (1979). *The Duke of Deception*. New York: Random House.

Wolkenfeld, F. (1985). Personal communication to Helen K. Gediman.

——— (1990). The parallel process phenomenon revisited: some additional thoughts about the supervisory process. In *Psychoanalytic Approaches to Supervision*, ed. R. C. Lane. New York: Brunner/Mazel.

CREDITS

INDEX